FIRE IN THE GROVE

FIRE IN THE GROVE

The Cocoanut Grove
TRAGEDY
and Its Aftermath

JOHN C. ESPOSITO

DA CAPO PRESS
A Member of the Perseus Books Group

Designed by Brent Wilcox
Set in 11.5 point Janson Text by the Perseus Books Group

Cataloging-in-Publication data for this book is available from the Library of Congress.

First Da Capo Press edition 2005
ISBN-10 0-306-81423-4
ISBN-13 978-0-306-81423-5

Published by Da Capo Press
A Member of the Perseus Books Group
http://www.dacapopress.com

Da Capo Press books are available at special discounts for bulk purchases in the U.S. by corporations, institutions, and other organizations. For more information, please contact the Special Markets Department at the Perseus Books Group, 11 Cambridge Center, Cambridge, MA 02142, or call (800) 255-1514 or (617) 252-5298, or email special.markets@perseusbooks.com.

1 2 3 4 5 6 7 8 9—09 08 07 06 05

To Linda and Nick, the flames in my heart

To firefighters and fire prevention professionals

Injustice is relatively easy to bear;
what stings is justice.

———————

H. L. Mencken

CONTENTS

ACKNOWLEDGMENTS

I owe debts of gratitude to a number of people who provided encouragement and assistance in the writing of this story.

First, my agent, Albert Zuckerman at Writers House, provided invariably shrewd advice about the structure of the book as well as about the publishing industry.

Among the people in Boston, Fire Commissioner Paul Christian, who opened his department's records of the Grove fire to me, helped immeasurably. Firefighter William Noonan, who has made the fire his special province, assisted me in wading through his vast archive of transcripts, news clippings, and photographs. Throughout the writing of this book, Bill promptly answered every email inquiry for clarification of some fine points.

William Arthur Reilly, son of the fire commissioner at the time of the fire, was generous with his time and provided invaluable insights about his father. I have made some stern judgments about the senior Mr. Reilly, but I hope that my essential respect for his performance after the fire is evident.

Dick Dray, Mr. Reilly's friend, was unfailingly generous with his time and contacts.

Author and *Boston Herald* reporter Stephanie Schorow, who has written extensively and well about the Grove and other Boston fires, provided helpful advice and materials.

I am indebted to several long-time friends for their support during the early lonely days: Daniel Weiss, Kay Gelfman, Bob

Henzler, Larry J. Silverman, Mark Adams, and Eric Bruce. I thank Anna La Violette for her boundless enthusiasm and Susan La Violette for her kindness. My special thanks go to Jamie Rosenthal Wolf for her unremitting interest and keen insights.

David Martinez created the Cocoanut Grove graphic that I believe is so helpful in understanding the club's layout.

Alison Sundet provided timely help with research.

Although I have never met him, I am grateful to Jack Beatty, author of *The Rascal King* (Da Capo Press, 2000). His excellent biography of James Michael Curley was a primary source of information about that political legend. In addition, I would recommend Barbara Ravage's *Burn Unit* (Da Capo Press, 2004) to readers interested in the development of modern treatment of burn injuries.

The capable staff at Da Capo Press has made the production of this book trouble-free: John Radziewicz, Kevin Hanover, Kate Adams, Sean Maher, Fred Francis, Erin Sprague, Matty Goldberg, Liz Tzetzo, Alex Camlin, Steve Cooley, and Jennifer Swearingen. I am particularly grateful to Dan O'Neil, my very thorough and competent editor.

I invite readers to visit the web site www.fireinthegrove.com for additional information and discussion about this book.

New York City, July 2005

Saturday Night, November 28, 1942

Park Square, Downtown Boston. The first fire alarm—from Box 1514 in Boston's theater and nightclub district—was struck at precisely 10:15 P.M.

It was a car fire.

Within minutes of the alarm, Deputy Chief Louis C. Stickel arrived in his fire department car at the corner of Stuart and Carver Streets. As he pulled his bulky frame out of his vehicle, Stickel saw that his men had already extinguished the small fire in a car parked near the corner of Broadway and Stuart. Most of the apparatus had been dismissed and the "all-out" signal ordered. Only one engine and one ladder truck remained. Stickel decided that nothing here required the presence of departmental brass on this chilly night.

He was about to slip back into the warmth of his automobile when a fireman looking past him down Broadway said, "You got another one going up over there, Chief."

Stickel turned and saw a large black cloud of smoke pushing skyward several hundred feet down Broadway. He ran down the street toward the second fire, the remnants of the engine company screaming by him.

Stickel and his men knew exactly where they were going. "I saw it was the Cocoanut Grove," he reported later.

Boston's legendary nightclub was burning.

The first thing Stickel saw through the thick smoke was a man's head and arm poking through an impossibly small hole in the thick glass block that had weeks before replaced the store window of the Grove's New Broadway Lounge. The firemen began smashing at the glass block to help the man, but the awful rush of smoke and heat pushed them back. Stickel ordered his men to play the hoses on the man, but it was too late. He could only watch as the water splashed ineffectually off the block onto the sidewalk. "And then a flame took him up," Stickel said.

At the end of this long night, Deputy Chief Stickel would learn that the fire had started nearly a city block away from where he watched that first death, at the farthest end of the jumble of buildings that made up the Cocoanut Grove nightclub.

He would also learn that by the time he had arrived at the scene—at 10:23 P.M.—that nameless man reaching out through the glass block was one of nearly five hundred people—one of every two persons on the premises—who were either already dead or doomed. Stickel was witness to the worst nightclub fire in American history.

It had all begun just eight minutes earlier, at 10:15, precisely when that coincidental car fire alarm had been turned in.

Phillips House, Massachusetts General Hospital. It was a coincidence, as well, that at 10:15 P.M. Grove owner Barnett C. Welansky was far from the object of his pride, joy, and considerable fortune. Until recently, it would have been difficult to remember a night when this portly little martinet was not prowling around his club, hovering about his bartenders, waiters, and cashiers, fussing over every detail. But tonight, the forty-five-year-old lawyer-turned-nightclub operator lay in a private room at Massachusetts General Hospital, where he had been rushed twelve days earlier after collapsing with a heart attack. Since then, his condition had been complicated by pneumonia, and on this Saturday night, it must have seemed to him that his recovery would be very slow—if it was to come at all.

Damn! Just when things were humming. Barney's physical discomfort must have been compounded by his bitterness. *Why me? Why now?*

Barney Welansky had acquired ownership of the club back in 1933, the year Prohibition had been repealed. In the nine years since, this determined man had turned the formerly gangster-run speakeasy into *the* hot spot for Boston's solid middle class. Certainly, the Grove was still a wild place by staid Boston's standards, with lavish floor shows and exotic décor, but it was now also a respectable establishment that was appropriate for anniversary parties, political dinners, and dates among the younger set. Cleansed of its sinister image and perhaps a bit tame compared to its speakeasy days, the Grove had been transformed by Welansky into a place where open-minded Boston WASPs could mix with the Irish, the Jews, and the Italians. Indeed, Bostonians from those groups and of that generation would for years recall that "everybody went there."

The war had increased business enormously. It had been almost a year since the Pearl Harbor attack, and wartime spending had thickened the wallets of the locals, just as the mobilization had swelled the population of Boston. The streets of the old port city were teeming with sailors, soldiers, and airmen, thousands of charged-up young men, far from home, fatalistic about the future and in search of a good time.

From his hospital bed, Barney could comfort himself in the knowledge that this was the long Thanksgiving weekend and the day of the Big Game, the annual football battle of the Jesuits—Boston College, the hometown favorite, and its archrival from Worcester, Holy Cross. It didn't matter very much that BC had lost. Barney knew that many Cocoanut Grove patrons had booked postgame parties and were unlikely to cancel. Mayor Tobin himself was to be at the Grove with Fire Commissioner Reilly to host a dinner for the players of both teams.

Barney knew there would be a thousand people in his club on that night—*easy.*

Business had not always been so good, Barney would have remembered, thinking back to the days when he had first "inherited" the Cocoanut Grove from the estate of his deceased law client, Charles Solomon. In January 1933, "King" Solomon was shot dead in the men's room of the Cotton Club, a mixed-race speakeasy in Boston's Roxbury section. Barney had become the estate's attorney.

"The estate didn't want it," Barney would later explain about his "inheritance," claiming that he had "spoken" to the probate judge, although there was barely a notation of the transaction in the court records. Why the King's estate "didn't want it" and what Welansky paid for it, if anything, would be one of the many secrets that Barney would take to his grave.

His client, Charlie Solomon, had been a tough and flashy gangster whose influence had extended throughout the New

England underworld. Charlie had been a charter member of "the Combination," the informal national board of directors of the Jewish wing of organized crime, whose "chairman" was New York's Meyer Lansky. King Solomon brought solid credentials to the Combination. At the time of his murder, the *Boston American* said Solomon "had reached the pinnacle of his fame as a dope peddler, panderer, grafter, loan shark, alky runner and New England czar of the popular forms of villainy."

Barney Welansky had always kept himself at a safe distance from such "villainy." Barney had been close enough personally to Solomon to have been one of the King's pallbearers, but professionally he handled only Solomon's straight-up business deals, including the King's purchase of the Grove in 1930. One couldn't have imagined the modest, soft-spoken Barney saying, "You'll pay for this—I'll have you put on the spot," as Solomon reportedly said to his killers just before he was plugged. Barney made an unlikely successor to the ostentatious Solomon, who had held court at the Grove every night, according to the *Boston American*, in his "skillfully tailored tuxedo fitted like a plaster mold." By contrast, Barney was pudgy and bald, wore rumpled suits, and had virtually no life outside of the Grove. By 1942, he no longer practiced law, choosing to devote his time to his beloved nightclub. His marriage was quiet and childless, and he demonstrated no interest in the Grove's pretty checkroom and chorus girls.

Barney might have been reserved, even bashful, but he was no wimp. "His word was everything," said Mickey Alpert, the club's master of ceremonies. But Barney was respected rather than feared—as Solomon had been.

Angelo Lippi, the club's longtime maître d', who had been cheated by the King on his paycheck every week but had been too frightened to complain, counted Barney a distinct improvement. "I'll say this for Barney, he never cut my pay," said Lippi. Barney may have seemed bland and frugal, but behind the colorless façade was a man of ambition, of business imagination, and even of some flair.

Business at the Grove was slow at first, even with the repeal of Prohibition. The Depression was biting hard in '33 and '34, and Welansky had to undo the years of Solomon's mismanagement. Although the King had been business-like about his rackets, he had run the club as a personal indulgence, valuing its limelight over its bottom line. Preoccupied with his far-flung criminal enterprises, he had no interest in the day-to-day management decisions, which he left to others. "That's just spit money," Solomon is reported to have said when he heard that the club was $30,000 in the red after his first year of ownership. By the time Barney took over, the place was a money pit.

In the nine years since the King's death, Welansky had built the modern Grove piece by piece. He transformed the unused spaces adjoining the original opulent 3,600-square-foot dining room into new venues for fun seekers. The club was now more than twice its original size, a 10,000-square-foot labyrinth of three rooms with four bars built on two levels, all woven together by steep staircases and twisting corridors.

Lying in his hospital bed, Barney could easily visualize that night's scene at the Grove. In the main dining room, the dance floor would be packed, and waiters would be carrying aloft extra tables and chairs as they searched for floor space. Barney could picture the steady flow of patrons through the revolving door of the main entrance and customers filling the foyer waiting for tables, squeezing into the adjoining forty-eight-foot-long Caricature Bar or filing down the staircase with the blue fabric ceiling to the "intimate" Melody Lounge in the basement.

Yeah, the place would be bursting at the seams . . . the money rolling in . . .

The most recent expansion, the New Broadway Lounge, had opened just eleven days earlier, the day after his heart attack, so Barney had never seen the room in operation. But his brother Jimmy, who had visited earlier in the evening, was watching the store in Barney's absence and had reported that business had been good from the first night.

The new room was unlike the older parts of the club, which had been done in a random concoction of jungle kitsch, a fantasy of Tahiti by way of the Arabian Nights, with lots of blue satin covering the ceilings above the club's signature imitation palm trees. Instead, the New Broadway Lounge was decorated in a crisp and tidy modern style, its neon-lined walls and scallop-shaped bar covered with glossy leatherette, its window that had looked out on Broadway refitted with that contemporary glass block.

Preparations for the new room had probably brought on the heart attack. Over the past several months, he had driven himself crazy fretting over every detail of the expansion and "negotiating" with those pests from the liquor licensing board about the tricky issue of installing expensive "fusible" fire doors between the old premises and the new. Fusible doors—doors that close automatically in case of fire—were not only expensive but would cut down on seating capacity.

Not to mention that municipal permits and inspections cost money. He had managed to expand the size of the club by two-and-a-half times its 1933 dimensions largely without the benefit of municipal approvals. However, he couldn't open the new room without a liquor license.

Thank God, Jimmy came through. On the very day of the opening, with Barney in the hospital, his brother had convinced Mary Driscoll, chair of the Boston licensing board, that everything was "according to Hoyle"—and she obligingly went for it, no questions asked. Barney got his liquor license hours before the opening of the new room, without installing the fire doors.

Building and fire codes were just a license for politicians to steal. They got enough from him already. The liquor license flap had been unusual, though. The authorities generally gave Barney no trouble. He understood the ways of Boston politics. All the big shots regularly stopped into the Cocoanut Grove. Some customers—politicians, newspapermen, bankers—had the best kind of "charge accounts"—the kind where no bills were ever rendered. For the privileged few, dinner or drink checks required only a scribbled authorization from the boss— "a good friend," "see me," "important," and "will settle later." These notations were also a good way to keep records of those who were beholden to him. Barney saved every free drink and dinner check.

Barney might have consoled himself that night by recalling how he had reinvented himself along with the Cocoanut Grove. He was now a respected Boston businessman with important connections to Mayor Tobin and other Boston politicians.

He had been born into a poor Russian-Jewish immigrant family, but he was now a wealthy man. In these all-cash, pre-credit-card days of 1942, he admitted to a weekly take of between five and six thousand dollars—better than a quarter million a year—several million in today's dollars. But beyond the money, he must have felt rich with pride and excitement over running so glamorous an enterprise.

But this damn heart attack had spoiled it, and tonight in his bed at Mass General, he was wondering if he would live or die. Barney had good reason to feel sorry for himself on this night. But he couldn't have realized at 10:15 P.M. that the worst was yet to come.

Parker House Hotel Dining Room. At 10:15 P.M., the only problem William Arthur Reilly had was helping to preside over a very glum "victory party." On this night, Reilly, Fire Commissioner of the City of Boston, and his boss, Mayor Maurice J. Tobin, were to have been at the Cocoanut Grove, but things had not gone according to plan.

Boston College had gone into this afternoon's game with a season record of 9 and 0, justifying the widespread expectation that it would be invited to play in the Sugar Bowl just as soon as it dispatched the mediocre Holy Cross team. Earlier that week, the *Boston Herald*'s sports columnist had written that BC was so formidable that "they should not be allowed to use more than six men at a time."

In a stunning upset, Holy Cross humiliated its rival, winning the game 55–12. There would be no Sugar Bowl invitation. Under the circumstances, Tobin and Reilly decided to pass on the boisterous Cocoanut Grove in favor of a quiet dinner at the sedate Parker House dining room for a scattering of the dispirited BC players as well as some members of the Holy Cross team.

The low-key mood abruptly shattered as word reached the commissioner that the Cocoanut Grove was burning. Reilly and

Tobin were soon in the mayor's limousine speeding south around the Boston Common to the nearby Grove.

Hearing the screeching sirens of fire trucks and ambulances coming from every direction, Reilly must have thought, *This has to be big.* He would later learn that by 10:24—nine minutes after the fire had started, and one minute after Deputy Chief Stickel's race down to the Broadway side of the club—a second, third, and fourth alarm had been turned in.

After quickly noting how lucky they had been to skip a night at the Cocoanut Grove, Reilly and Tobin, the two most powerful city politicians, must have quickly taken stock, their hushed conversation repeatedly circling around a number of important questions.

- *Who's in charge?* Reilly was a politician and businessman with no fire-fighting background. Department Chief Samuel J. Pope would be in charge, and he was a good man, an experienced professional firefighter.
- *What about inspections?* Reilly's people did the routine fire inspections, and the building department was supposed to look after structure and exits. The Boston licensing board was to confer—sort of confer, nobody was quite sure—with the fire and building departments before issuing liquor licenses. That stuff had better be in order.
- *What about the Welanskys?* Mayor Tobin's association with Barney and Jimmy Welansky was well known. The brothers were "contributors," and the mayor could be found almost every night downing his Canadian Club and chain-smoking at Jimmy's Circle Lounge Bar at Cleveland

Circle. Just weeks ago, the mayor had appointed Barney to the War Resources Board.

Reilly became fire commissioner in 1938, after managing Tobin's upstart first campaign against their erstwhile mentor and patron, the legendary James Michael Curley. Curley was the thinly veiled model for the central character of Edwin O'Conner's *The Last Hurrah*, the novel about a corrupt, beguiling mayor of Boston, governor of Massachusetts, congressman, and political boss.

The real James Michael Curley—once described as a man who could have become president of the United States if only he had been honest—had maintained his power since the World War I era by relentlessly stoking the bitterness of the Irish. Not many generations before, the native Protestant population had welcomed the new arrivals with "Irish Need Not Apply" signs in factory and store windows and with newspaper cartoons and commentary depicting the new immigrants as staggering under the twin burdens of popery and alcoholism—the "Irish flu."

Curley, perhaps the inventor of American identity politics, reminded the Irish of this rude greeting at every opportunity. "The Anglo-Saxon is a joke," Curley told his constituents. "A new and better America is here."

No single immigrant group has ever overwhelmed an American city to the extent that the Irish had Boston. Long before 1942, the nonpartisan municipal elections had come down to choosing from among Democrats with names like Hurley, Curley, Kerrigan, and Tobin. However, while the Irish may have run Boston, they did not own it. The politically displaced Protestant, Republican old guard was still in firm control of the banks, insurance companies, cultural institutions, and newspapers. Long-reconciled to its minority status, the Yankee establishment now contented itself with anointing and supporting the "better elements" among the Irish: the reformist (that is, anti-Curley), college-educated, upwardly mobile, "lace-curtain" or "two-toilet" Irish.

As Boston's mayoral election of 1937 rolled around, the Yankees trembled at the specter of Curley, who had been out of public office since losing his senatorial bid a year earlier, reclaiming the mayor's office for a fourth time in three decades. To beat the old fraud back, Boston's "better elements" rallied around the more polished, more malleable Maurice (pronounced Morris) J. Tobin.

Tobin was an attractive, new-style Irish politician who fit the bill perfectly, despite his Mission Hill working-class roots. He was well spoken, tall, and blessed with delicate good looks. Curley had brought Tobin and his good friend Reilly along in politics in the early '30s. However, the two decided that their political fortunes would improve by distancing themselves from their sponsor.

During the 1937 campaign, the *Boston Post* lauded Tobin as "the candidate of the forces which offer the one chance of redemption of the city." Seizing his chance, and with William Arthur Reilly's guidance and connections, Tobin turned on his much-tarnished mentor.

Wearing the mantle of the reform candidate, Tobin beat Curley twice, once in 1937 and again in 1941, helped in no small measure by Reilly's resources and influence.

After Tobin's first victory, Reilly had chosen the fire department as his prize because it offered maximum positive exposure for his own political career. Although he lacked Tobin's movie-star looks, he nevertheless cut an authoritative and elegant figure in his politician's uniform of the era—carefully tailored suit, homburg hat, and chesterfield coat. He was an important member of the Clover Club—the Irish answer to the Somerset Club and other Yankee-dominated men's clubs—a Boston College graduate, and reasonably affluent. He had inherited a Catholic music publishing business from his father.

Reilly's father had gone into the business with the special blessing of Joseph Cardinal O'Connell, the bishop of Boston. Because of the influence of the Boston church among American Catholics, the firm of McLaughlin and Reilly had a virtual monopoly over printed church music and over seminarians' materials distributed throughout the country.

Reilly inherited the business from his father, which gave him two important resources for a Boston politician—an independent income and access to a network of Boston priests, nuns, and engaged Catholic laypeople.

It must have been clear to both men that they were going places. Tobin's next stop was the governor's office. The chances were perfect for Reilly to succeed him as mayor—until this particular Saturday night, perhaps.

As they reached the club, Reilly saw that the narrow streets around the Grove were already clogged with more emergency vehicles than he had ever seen at one fire. Smoke and flames were everywhere. Firefighters, policemen, military men on leave, and passersby were climbing over each other in their desperate efforts to pull patrons out of the burning building. What looked like hundreds of bodies—the dying and dead—were piled chest-high on icy sidewalks.

Reilly watched, horror-struck, as firemen with axes hacked away at locked emergency exit doors and the hysterical victims who made it out of the Grove alive staggered about, dazed or screaming for friends and loved ones still trapped inside.

It would be the fire commissioner's statutory duty to investigate and report to the public on this fire. This would be tricky.

First, there was Mayor Tobin's association with the Welansky brothers. Second, Reilly knew that his own Fire Prevention Bureau was responsible for certain inspections of the premises. Other agencies—the building department, the police department, and the Boston licensing board, all run by the inner circle of local politicians—were each to a degree responsible for the safety of the premises and their customers.

But more than any of those others, even more than the mayor himself, Reilly would be in the spotlight over this. He would have to answer some tough questions.

When offered his choice of city posts, Reilly had considered the fire department to be the plum job. Now he knew he had made a mistake.

Newton, Massachusetts.   Robert Tyng Bushnell, the Republican Massachusetts state attorney general, was at home and not at his office at the State House in downtown Boston on this Saturday night, but he would have learned quickly that the Cocoanut Grove was burning.

He must have taken grim satisfaction at the terrible news. He knew this day of retribution was coming. He had, in a way, seen it coming.

Although not a native Bostonian, having been born into well-to-do circumstances in New York, the forty-six-year-old Bushnell shared the Yankees' puritanical fury over political corruption. He was a Phillips Andover and Harvard man who would have been comfortable living at the time Massachusetts was ruled by the Puritans, who had defined themselves by their antipathy to popery.

But the attorney general fell short of the stereotype of the stoic, reserved Yankee patrician. He was notorious for public fits of temper, a slashing courtroom manner, and over-the-top rhetorical flourishes. As a rising star in the Republican Party, Bushnell had lamented the twin misfortunes that the voters of the state had brought upon themselves in the 1935 elections; they had simultaneously elected James Michael Curley as governor and legalized dog racing. Bushnell saw a parallel.

"The poor beasts," he had said, "trained in puppy hood to mangle the bodies of live rabbits and later kept at a point of starvation so that they will dash blindly and hungrily after a fake rabbit, are in precisely the same situation as the voters of Massachusetts."

Stocky and kinetic, with a wild head of hair and a Thomas E. Dewey–like mustache, the attorney general may in fact have modeled himself on the New York crime-busting prosecutor who had become the symbol of reform of the nation's corrupt cities.

Now it might be Bushnell's turn for the national spotlight, thanks to this dreadful fire.

Until this night, Bushnell had been preoccupied with his secret investigation into the ties between Police Commissioner Joseph Timilty, a former Curley campaign manager, and one Dr. Harry J. Sagansky.

"Doc Jasper," as Sagansky was known to friends and associates, had long ago abandoned his Scollay Square dental practice

to preside over a $90 million numbers racket. Bushnell had
drawn the obvious conclusion that a racket whose base of operations was across the street from the Charlestown police station
could not have operated without the connivance of the police
commissioner. Sagansky and Timilty were just the types Bushnell despised. The first was an out-and-out crook, while the second was a corrupt official contemptuous of public trust and
defiling Bushnell's ideal of the Holy Commonwealth, a community of the righteous presided over by the most righteous.

Now Bushnell was presented with the opportunity to unravel
the sordid ties between the nightclub operators and the city's
politicians. His mind must have raced through the names of
those involved:

- Barney Welansky, the fellow who had been that gangster's
  lawyer;
- Mayor Maurice Tobin, who seemed more the clever Curley
  protégé than a reformer;
- those political types, William Arthur Reilly at the fire department, James H. Mooney at the building department,
  and Mary Driscoll at the licensing board.

They would all have to answer.

The Sunday morning papers, which carried the shocking stories of the fire, also provided the citizenry with Bushnell's first
discourse on the tragedy: The flames at the Cocoanut Grove and
the flames of corruption charring Boston were one and the same.

Bushnell's crusade for the redemption of Boston began November 28, 1942.

CHAPTER 1

The Rehearsal

City "Blasted" in Its Biggest Daytime Raid

Boston Herald *front-page headline,*
Monday, November 23, 1942

O N THE BRISK, sunny afternoon of November 22, 1942, Boston tested its preparedness by subjecting itself to a mock Luftwaffe attack. In the city's tidy response to this imaginary foreign assault, fire-fighting equipment sped to simulated fire scenes, physicians and nurses reported to staged incidents, and laundry trucks became ambulances rushing to remove the "injured" to area hospitals. At the end of this exercise, only 23 persons were declared "dead" while 300 were "wounded." It had all gone precisely as planned, said Mayor Maurice Tobin, and he declared the citywide drill a success. What in fact had occurred was an unwitting dry run for the city's worst domestic catastrophe that came less than a week later.

This mock assault was no academic exercise. As the nation approached the first anniversary of the Pearl Harbor attack, there were nightly reminders that the homeland itself was threatened. Most of the Massachusetts coast—from Cape Cod Bay in the south to Sailsbury in the north—was subject to "dimout regulations," restrictions on street and house lights to protect from air assault. Everyone took seriously the possibility of air attack, sabotage, or even invasion—and for good reason. The war was not going well in November 1942.

There had already been small-scale invasions of U.S. territory. Earlier in the year, German saboteurs had been dropped by U-boats onto the coasts of Florida and Long Island, New York. Moreover, the Japanese controlled Kiska and Attu, American islands in the Aleutian chain off the Alaskan mainland. Across the Pacific, the British had lost Singapore in February, and U.S. forces had surrendered the Philippines in May. In Europe, the Germans had been besieging Stalingrad for four months. In North Africa, the Allied invasion that had begun on November 8 was meeting stiff resistance in Tunisia.

By November, the war had disrupted nearly every aspect of American life. President Roosevelt had just announced that 600,000 young men would be drafted between December 11 and 31. Ultimately, sixteen million Americans would serve in the war. Henceforth, every American boy would be required to register on his eighteenth birthday.

The president had also signed orders authorizing the recruitment of women into the Women's Army Auxiliary Corps, the "WAAC," or its naval counterpart, the WAVES. All told, by the war's end, 265,000 women would serve. These female volunteers released men for the battlefront by engaging is all manner of backup jobs—clerks, bakers, bookkeepers, and dispatchers. The government had announced that enrollment was open to all twenty-one to forty-four-year-old women "regardless of race, creed, or color."

A spirit of universal sacrifice and service prevailed. Because of its coastal position, Boston was overflowing with sailors and coastguardsmen. Older men and women of all ages were volunteers, selling war bonds and acting as public safety wardens, Red Cross aides, or USO hostesses. Slattery's department store pleaded for used silk and nylon stockings (washed) to make into powder bags.

Children, too, were expected to do their part. Kraft Foods offered a booklet instructing youngsters on ways to help at home so that parents would have more time to devote to the war effort. The *Boston Traveler* called on all Junior Commandos to come to the big rally at Boston Garden on Saturday morning, November 28. The kids, who would be encouraged at the rally to save their pennies to buy war stamps, were promised, "You'll see the Marching Marines, you'll hear the stirring music of the famed Army and Navy bands, and you'll applaud Buck Jones, the cowboy movie star." After his daylong series of patriotic events, Buck Jones would spend his Saturday night at the Cocoanut Grove.

Every Boston paper carried want ads for skilled and unskilled men and women to work at premium wartime wages at such defense sites as the Hingham or Lawley shipyards or the Sikorsky Air Craft Corporation. The ads promised that unskilled workers would be "paid while they learn." In order to discourage job shopping, applicants were warned that they could not be considered for these positions if they were already employed in war work.

To protect against inflation, hoarding, and shortages, nearly all prices were fixed by the federal Office of Price Administration

(OPA). Cities in turn established local war resources boards to coordinate with the OPA. Missing no opportunity to bestow patronage at no cost, Mayor Tobin had recently appointed Cocoanut Grove owner Barnett C. Welansky to the Boston board. Department store ads entreated customers to "shop only in stores which post ceiling prices and cooperate with the OPA." Salaries were capped at $67,500.00, but few people were in so heady an income bracket. Nevertheless, with wartime jobs paying higher than normal wages, and with many factories operating at full throttle twenty-four hours a day, overtime pay was routine. Bostonians were doing well, but they were admonished to avoid lavish spending. "Foolish Spending Is Treason," warned a dour Uncle Sam in an announcement sponsored by the mutual savings banks of Massachusetts.

In early November, the OPA announced that gasoline and home heating fuel allocations would be reduced. In response, the Massachusetts health department offered tips on staying warm, including going to bed early and elevating one's feet when seated. Filene's department store saw the bright side to rubber and gasoline shortages in the opportunity to do "tireless shopping" by taking the subway downtown. Scarce supplies of gasoline and tires had another advantage; less driving meant lower insurance rates. The Massachusetts Department of Insurance announced that the maximum compulsory insurance premium in 1943 would be $43.00, down from $53.70 for 1942.

Advertisers demonstrated a superb ingenuity in tying their promotions to the war effort and patriotism. Imported White Horse scotch whiskey proudly announced, "Every bottle has won a battle to get here." Florsheim Shoes was pleased "to have put America on a healthful footing," thus reducing the loss of "priceless man hours." Even toilet paper manufacturers managed to find a war theme: "War Bonds—Victory Insurance, Statler Toilet Tissue—Health Insurance." The Jordan Marsh department store advertised its "Victory-Rite Kit" for servicemen (at $1.95), which included seventy-five "men's size" letter sheets, with appropriate service insignias, twenty-four no-postage postcards, blotters, envelopes, and a desk-top writing box. Camel cigarettes ($1.54 per carton at the Stop and Shop Super-Market) told readers that it was "First in the Service . . . based on actual sales records in canteens and post exchanges." The Necco candy company—"In the service of the Service"— pictured cartooned service members announcing, "Sky Bar is My Bar." The White Owl Cigar Company apologized for its recent price increase to six cents a cigar, "but this is wartime, with higher costs all along the line." The company solemnly promised to return to its pre-war five-cent level "at the earliest moment that costs make it possible."

War themes pervaded public entertainment. Irving Berlin appeared at the Boston Opera House in his traveling all-soldier show, *This Is the Army*. The diminutive songwriter, dressed in his World War I uniform, reportedly brought the crowd to its feet when he sang "Oh How I Hate to Get Up in the Morning." On the night of the fire, a number of cast members would stop in the Cocoanut Grove to have a drink before their show and have their pictures taken with Grove emcee Mickey Alpert.

George White's Scandals of 1943, opening a month in advance of the New Year at the RKO Boston, featured the "24 George White Beauties." According to the *Boston Herald*'s female reviewer, the Beauties didn't have much to do "but walk around . . . remove some of their clothes . . . and sing such songs as 'I Said Yes' to bashful but obviously well-pleased soldiers and sailors."

The war topped the best-seller lists. The top three best-selling nonfiction books in Boston in late 1942 were *See Here, Private Hargrove*, a humorous look at basic training; *They Were Expendable*, the drama of a torpedo boat squadron's grim experience during the Philippine debacle; and *Suez to Singapore*, a CBS war correspondent's firsthand account of the brutal fighting in the Malaysian jungle and the fall of Singapore. (J. K. Lasser's *Your Income Tax, 1943* was fourth on the list.)

Movie fare ranged between propaganda and escapism. Opening just in time for the Thanksgiving holiday at the Paramount and Fenway was *Flying Tigers*—"The First Yanks to Blast the Japs"— starring John Wayne. Held over for a third week—"So that all Boston May See How America Is Dishing It Out to the Axis"— was *The Navy Comes Through*, starring Pat O'Brien and George Murphy. Those who wanted escape could go to the Egyptian and see Abbott and Costello in *Pardon My Sarong*, or to the Metropolitan to see Crosby, Hope, and Lamour in *Road to Morocco*.

Nevertheless, Bostonians anticipated an austere Thanksgiving holiday. Governor Saltonstall asked defense workers to stay on the job during the holiday to avoid breaks in production. Railroads warned of limited passenger schedules to accommodate war traffic. Turkey was expensive at forty-nine cents a pound, and coffee and sugar sales had been halted completely, pending the start of rationing of those commodities on Saturday, November 28.

Between the high costs and rationing of commodities, a better deal might be had at one of Boston's restaurants. Thanksgiving dinner cost $3.00 at the Hotel Vendome (which would burn and collapse in 1972, killing nine firemen); at the Hi-Hat it ran $2.50; or for just $2.00, one could enjoy a full-course dinner at the Rio Casino as well as the "sensational revue featuring Diosa Costello, the Puerto Rican Tornado." At the sober high end, Thanksgiving dinner in the main dining room of the Parker House cost $3.50.

Boston's major league sports teams were in crisis because of the war. Although FDR had recently issued his "Green Light" letter, encouraging major leagues to continue their operations through the war, owners of the Boston Red Sox, Braves, and Bruins seriously worried whether there would be a 1943 baseball or hockey season. The Sox had ten players in the service, most notably their star, Ted Williams, who had volunteered. The ranks of the Braves were similarly depleted by the draft and enlistment. Team owners considered that they might employ seventeen-year-olds or older men with families. The National Hockey League suspended the minimum player rule—twelve men plus a goalie—for the duration of the war.

Manpower shortages also affected the Boston fire department. Several days before Thanksgiving, Commissioner William Arthur Reilly appealed to local selective service system boards to defer the drafting of firefighters for at least six months. The department had already lost 130 men to the draft, he said. In addition, the department's ranks had been further depleted less than two weeks earlier when six firemen had been killed and forty-two hospitalized as a result of the building collapse at the Luongo's Restaurant fire.

Not all of the city's planning was as high profile as its very public disaster drill. After the horror of the Pearl Harbor attack, the government had come to understand that this would be a "burns war" for which the military and the medical community were ill prepared. Remarkably little was known in 1942 about the efficient treatment of burn injuries, especially on a large scale. Consequently, the National Research Council had turned earlier in the year to two of the city's preeminent hospitals— Boston City and Massachusetts General—to study burn treatment with a particular view to developing procedures to care for massive burn casualties under battle conditions. By November, both hospitals were unusually well prepared to deal with a large-scale fire catastrophe—an event that everyone believed would be initiated by a foreign enemy.

CHAPTER 2

The Intimate Place

The building was not one which the layman would have
considered a fire trap.

"The Cocoanut Grove Fire,"
Report of the National Fire Protection Association,
January 11, 1943

I T WAS ALWAYS MIDNIGHT in the Melody Lounge.
In fact, the popular joke about the Cocoanut Grove's basement bar was that you had to strike a match to find your drink,
and this wasn't far from the truth. Except for one indirect light in
the center of the ceiling and some neons glowing from beneath
the bar, all the light in the intimate Melody Lounge came from a
scattering of 7½-watt bulbs. These tiny specks of illumination
flickered dimly though the motionless fronds of the imitation
palm trees placed in the corners of the room. No more powerful
than Christmas tree lights, the bulbs were set into the laminated
coconut husks that had been screwed to the trunks.

During Prohibition, the sale of alcohol was theoretically illegal, so the original Grove had no bar. In late 1933, Barney Welansky lost no time in taking advantage of repeal and built two

bars in the club: the plush Caricature Bar on the main floor, adjoining the original main dining room, and the more modest Melody Lounge, which he cobbled out of an old storage cellar. The Caricature Bar offered patrons a view of the stage show in the original club area, so it had to be up to main-floor standards. This 48-foot-long ritzy red leatherette-padded bar was still under construction in December 1933, when for the first time in thirteen years it was legal to serve alcohol. Angelo Lippi, the club's maître d'—nicknamed the Count for his elegant bearing— announced to the assembled revelers, "My dear ladies and gentlemen, it is my sublime pleasure to inform you, the bar is open." The Caricature Bar was a success from day one.

However, the Melody Lounge was a different story. Barney had at first moved tentatively in creating it, as he had been unsure how customers might respond to a bar in the cheerless basement, far away from the dance floor and the entertainment. He marshaled his stable of occasional workmen to build a small bar and a staircase from the main floor down to the basement and to disguise the masonry walls with cheap wood paneling.

In 1936, as business improved, Barney had the bar enlarged. By 1940, business had improved to the point where Barney had decided to go all-out with his third and most extensive renovation; he expanded the bar to a 35-by-18-foot octagon that covered about one-third of the floor space.

Despite the fact that he had not bothered to apply to the building department for permits on these three substantial renovations—a requirement of the Boston licensing board for a liquor license, at least in theory—Barney's existing license was quietly extended to cover the Melody Lounge and renewed annually thereafter. There had been no finicky inspector to deal with during those years—no bureaucratic unpleasantness like the aggravation over the New Broadway Lounge's fusible fire doors that had occurred more recently.

Barney had been just as masterful in meeting the marketing challenges created by the basement watering hole. The Melody Lounge was billed as a bar, pure and simple—no fancy food and no lavish floor shows, just a singer/piano player. Alcohol has always been the easiest money in the restaurant business—no waste, low overhead, and about a 400 percent markup. If you wanted to spring for a dinner and show in the original dining room upstairs, good for you, and better for Barney. But down in the Melody Lounge, you bought a bunch of tickets—a minimum of two bucks worth per person—and redeemed them for scotch and sodas, seven-and-sevens, or highballs. The beauty of the tickets-for-drinks system was that Barney didn't have to keep watch over everyone in the joint; bartenders and bar boys handled little cash except for their own tips.

It was a sweet system. Nevertheless, just to be on the safe side, Barney had recently installed his favorite nephew as the weekend undercover "checker" to keep a watchful eye on the cashiers and everyone else.

With the second renovation in 1936, Barney had decided to pull out all the stops and called in Reuben O. Bodenhorn, who had designed the original Cocoanut Grove up on the street floor in 1927. The makeshift Melody Lounge needed dressing up. The resourceful Bodenhorn cleverly met the design challenge of camouflaging this windowless basement by making its limitations the source of its allure. It would remain a dark space, a retreat of "umbrageous" intimacy, as Welansky's lawyers would later so elegantly describe it.

It was a tribute to Bodenhorn's flair that, by 1942, one couldn't think of the Melody Lounge without thinking of the word "intimate." Mostly, however, it was dark and crammed with the stuff of make-believe.

The low cement ceiling of this former garage building intensified the "intimacy" of the room. Only about 10 feet from the ground, the ceiling was effectively made still lower by 1,966 square feet of dark blue satin fabric suspended on wood strapping 12 to 18 inches below the cement. This suspended fabric, which according to designer Bodenhorn created "an illusion of the heavens on a starry night," also covered the ceiling of the staircase that led to and from the main floor.

The steep, fifteen-step staircase was the public's only way into and out of the Melody Lounge. Customers reached the top of the staircase by making an awkward 50-foot U-turn on the club's main floor. After pushing through the revolving door upstairs, the club's main entranceway on Piedmont Street, patrons walked into the foyer area about 12 feet, then turned to the left around an office/checkroom about 28 feet, then left again through a 10-foot corridor to the top of the staircase.

After making the long U-turn and walking down the fifteen steps, customers were transported from the gray streets of Boston to a world that existed only in the fantasy of Hollywood movies. If the harsh glare of daylight could have penetrated this windowless basement room, its trappings would no doubt have seemed gaudy and flimsy, especially to the modern eye. But at the beginning of the 1940s, in dowdy Boston, the underlit, exotic atmosphere evoked visions of Rogers and Astaire dancing in Rio or Morocco—and all points warm and balmy.

Rogers and Astaire would have ended their dance number by flopping on the wrap-around, zebra-striped settees that lined the walls. The walls above—as well as the staircase walls—had faux-cane leatherette covering with rattan and bamboo accents. The staircase had the additional touch of fish netting. The octagonal bar, also trimmed in rattan and bamboo, dominated the center of the room. The little floor area left between the bar and the settees was crowded with tables and chairs. Within the bar area, a piano was mounted on a revolving platform. On November 28, 1942, the singer-piano player, backlit by the neon glow from under the bar, was the portly Miss "Goodie" Goodell.

"Faintly lit" . . . "romantic" . . . "intimate"—the Melody Lounge was the perfect place for a guy to make the move on his date. And so John Bradley, the lounge's head bartender, paid no mind when, a few minutes before 10:15 P.M., he made out through the haze of cigarette smoke the twin silhouettes of a soldier warming up to his girl. The couple was seated on one end of the settee in the corner, just next to one of the palm trees with the illuminated coconut husks. The soldier was persistent—all arms and hands—but the girl seemed shy, the twinkle from the tiny bulb apparently too much like a spotlight for her comfort.

Bradley was too busy to watch for very long. He turned his attention back to the patrons standing three and four deep on all sides of his octagonal bar and to supervising the bar boys who shuttled drinks to the customers tightly packed onto the settees and at the additional tables on the floor.

There had been a steady stream of traffic up and down the staircase for a couple of hours. Some of the customers were listening to the songs of Goodie Goodell from atop her revolving platform. Others were talking over the music or drifting up the stairs to catch a dance in the main room, to see about getting a table, or to watch the floor show from the vantage of the Caricature Bar, the dining room's next-door neighbor.

Eventually, everyone went upstairs to use the rest rooms, as there were none downstairs.

But as the evening wore on, more people arrived than left. By 10:15 P.M., there could have been as many as four hundred people in this 35-by-55-foot room, with most of the floor space taken up by the bar, the tables, chairs, and settees.

But the Grove was always packed on Saturday nights. Given the cramped quarters, the guests at the Melody Lounge were more or less patient about delays in being served. Most customers seemed to understand that the bar boys had to work hard to navigate through the crowd at the bar and around the obstacle course created by the extra tables and chairs set out to accommodate as many as possible.

Sigmund Cohen was one of the impatient ones. He had come down to the Melody a few minutes after 10 P.M., intending to kill some time until the floor show began upstairs. But Cohen, not caring for the scene, decided to leave almost immediately.

"The place was packed and the smoke so thick," he remarked afterward. Despite being disturbed by the intense cigarette smoke, Cohen called over to the Grove's cigarette girl, Bunny Leslie, and bought a pack of his own. Then he headed upstairs. Instead of waiting inside, however, Sigmund pushed out through the revolving door in the upstairs foyer, lit up, and waited on Piedmont Street for the show to begin. "Something seemed to be in the air that made me do that," Cohen would say later with the certainty of hindsight.

Head barman John Bradley carried on downstairs. Things were going as well as could be expected. Very few seemed to be crying in their beers over BC's loss, and the mood was upbeat and friendly. Just as Goodie Goodell began to sing the latest Bing Crosby hit, "White Christmas," Bradley turned again to look at the corner where he'd seen the soldier and his shy girl. It was pitch black over there! *That soldier must have futzed with the light in the palm tree!* More darkness was the last thing the Melody Lounge needed, and John bent over the bar to tell sixteen-year-old bar boy Stanley Tomaszewski to get over to that corner and *get that light back on—now.*

Bradley's simple and well-intentioned instruction to Stanley went unnoticed by the patrons, who like bar patrons everywhere, were wrapped up in their own thoughts and plans for the evening.

For instance, twenty-one-year-old Joyce Spector and her fiancé Justin Morgan hadn't noticed that the light had gone out, although they were just one table away from the ardent soldier and his girl. At first, they had been put off by the slow service, but then they had become distracted by the conversation of the couple seated at the table shoehorned next to theirs. Joyce and Justin smiled to each other as they listened in. "It was their 25th wedding anniversary," Joyce would remember later. She recalled that he was "a nice little man" and thought "they didn't look like folks who went to nightclubs very often."

A couple of tables away, Navy Ensign William T. Connery and Lieutenant David Fretchling also didn't notice the darkened corner. They had gotten to the Melody Lounge a little after 10 and immediately zeroed in on a couple of girls standing at the bar, about 10 feet from the darkened palm tree. After a few minutes, Fretchling, apparently bored, made his excuses and said that he was going upstairs to look for some buddies. Connery decided to hang out with the girls and try to get a drink, which he had been unable to do for nearly fifteen minutes because the place was so packed.

Ruth and Hyman Strogoff were Wednesday and Saturday night regulars. Tonight they were sitting across the room from the soldier and his girl, perched at the bar about 3 feet from the staircase. They had been there about a half hour and felt lucky to get the two stools that friends had saved for them. Ruth called up to Goodie Goodell and told her to join them for a drink at the end of her set.

Seated at a table not far from the Strogoffs, close to the foot of the stairs, and almost diagonally across the room from the darkened corner, Coast Guard Gunner's Mate James W. Lane and his friend, Marine Private Donald W. Lauer, were just taking in the scene.

Next to Lane and Lauer was an attractive young foursome. Nathan Greer, a Harvard student from Santa Fe, was with his date, Kathleen O'Neil, a bank employee from Brookline. With them were Nathan's friend Jim Jenkins, captain of the Harvard tennis team, and Jim's pretty date, Ann McCardle, a prep school student. They had come to the Grove at about 9:30 and had decided to forego the crowd waiting to be seated in the main dining room by heading down to the Melody Lounge.

After about three-quarters of an hour, Ann excused herself to go upstairs to the ladies' room. Seconds later, Nathan's eye fell on the tableau across the room. "Somebody was tampering with the light," he said later, "I guess putting this bulb in."

It was Stanley Tomaszewski. Following Bradley's instructions, the young man had walked over to the soldier and, in his unfailingly polite manner, reminded him that turning off the light was dangerous. "It is rather dark here, and the few lights we have help keep you safe," he admonished the soldier.

Stanley looked into the darkened tree for the loosened bulb. He couldn't find it, and the soldier was not about to help. So Stanley stood on a bar stool and lit a match. Finding the darkened husk near the top, Stanley put the match in his right hand and tightened the bulb with his left. Then he blew out the match, stepped off the stool, dropped the extinguished match to the floor, and stepped on it.

Mission accomplished. It was 10:15 P.M.

As Stanley turned to walk back to his station across the room, someone shouted, "Hey, there's a fire in the palm tree." Stanley turned and saw that a few of the tree's imitation fronds near the top were crackling with flame. He walked back to the tree and pulled at it, trying to keep the fire away from the wall and ceiling. John Bradley ran from behind his bar to help, and he and Stanley tugged at the burning tree, which had been lashed to the ceiling to secure it.

> *"The fire originated in the Melody Lounge. . . . It was first seen burning in a palm tree."*
>
> Report Concerning the Cocoanut Grove Fire, Boston Fire Department, November 19, 1943

Other employees immediately joined Stanley and John Bradley around the tree, pulling at it and throwing pitchers of water on the fire. At first, those who even noticed what was going on were amused.

Donald Jeffers and his wife were celebrating their wedding anniversary. They'd had dinner at the Statler just around the corner and then had come to the Cocoanut Grove, just as they'd done on their wedding night eleven years earlier. Don remembered that they were standing very close to the "tiny blaze" and that "they were all laughing and joking" while the Grove employees wrestled with the burning tree, like Keystone Kops in white shirts and aprons.

It might not have been much of a fire, but there may never have been so much light in the Melody Lounge.

Joyce Spector and Justin Morgan, the eavesdropping couple, were neither amused nor overly alarmed. Nevertheless, already unhappy about the overflow crowd and the slow service, they decided that they could do without this little comic drama. Joyce was worried about her brand-new $800 leopardskin coat, which was in the checkroom on the main floor. She told Justin that she was going to go on ahead, collect her coat, and meet him upstairs. "It was just a little fire then, you understand," she would later recall with a trace of guilt.

> *"The fire immediately spread through the Melody Lounge along the underside of the false ceiling."*
>
> *Boston Fire Department Report*

Nathan Greer, his date Kathleen O'Neil, and Jim Jenkins also got up and started up the stairs. "I thought it would be a small fire," Nathan said later, "but my friend and I took no chances."

The smell of smoke distracted Ensign Bill Connery from his conversation with the two girls he'd just met, although just barely. He turned to see the excited staff attacking the flare-up about 10 feet away from him. Not concerned enough to leave the room yet, he continued chatting, but something told him to scan the room for an alternate exit to the public staircase he and Fretchling had come down.

It was about 10:16.

It took just seconds for the anxious staff to pull down the burning tree. "But it was too late, too far gone," barman Bradley would later say. His hands and face burned, Bradley looked up to see that the fabric ceiling immediately above the tree was sizzling.

Gunner's Mate Lane later said that he and his friend Don Lauer saw "a flame about the size of a dinner plate" flashing between the top of the tree and the blue satin suspended over it. However, the fire knew where it wanted to go—toward the oxygen-filled staircase. Almost immediately, the blue, orange, and yellow flame blossomed sideways and forward as it made its wedged-shaped march to the side walls and to the staircase— and directly at Lane and Lauer.

Don Lauer jumped on a chair and tried to deprive the fire of fuel by cutting at the "topside" with his pocketknife, said Lane. But the fire's burning path was moving too quickly. It zipped over their heads, now feeding on the fabric-covered ceiling of the staircase.

In seconds, the whole of Melody Lounge's starry heaven had turned into a crackling, spitting sheet of flame. It seemed to Ruth Strogoff that almost no time had elapsed between seeing the burning fronds and when "blue and orange flames were shooting in all different directions. You would be standing in one place and before you knew it, it would shoot out of another place." The flames were over everybody's head, spitting down on them, as though the Melody Lounge patrons were under a broiler.

There were panicked screeches and shouts for help, as the fire's destruction was fueled by the flimsy fabric of the ceiling. Large shreds of smoldering fabric were falling. The covering along the upper portion of the walls had started burning. The windowless room was filled with a dense black, acrid smoke. It was impossible to see the faces of nearby companions, or even to breathe.

Ensign Connery's hair was aflame. He spun around while beating at his head, and then he felt Stanley Tomaszewski's hands flailing at him to help extinguish the flames. Connery, who had started warily searching for another exit when the fire was still in the tree, had spotted the kitchen door on the back wall. The door was cut out of the wood paneling that made up the back wall and then hinged in place. Only the most observant could tell there was a door there. This door was close to where the fire had begun, but opposite the staircase, where it was heading.

Stanley directed Connery and some others through that kitchen door, but as the fire rolled across the ceiling, most of the frightened patrons, stumbling over upturned tables and chairs, pressed toward that familiar staircase diagonally across from the palm tree. The staircase was how they'd come. It was the only exit most knew.

Hundreds of people would have to race the flash fire up the narrow staircase. "There was [another] way to the street," said John Bradley, describing another exit behind the nearly imperceptible kitchen door. "But they were all hollering and screaming, and I don't think anyone thought about it," including Bradley himself.

But not everyone was running. Ruth Strogoff remembered that some "people were screaming but they seemed to be falling down without even trying to run or push. They dropped off stools."

These people were suffocating. Some were falling victim to the carbon monoxide in the thick smoke that was rapidly replacing the oxygen in their bloodstream. Others were burning up *inside* as they inhaled the superheated air—burning wood and fabric can generate temperatures of 1,800 degrees Fahrenheit—that seared shut their throats and lungs.

By about 10:17 everyone in the room not taken down by the smoke and flames was scrambling to escape. Ruth Strogoff was certain that she and Hyman were among the first to reach the staircase after the fire spread across the ceiling. But those behind them pulled at them in their own frenzied efforts to escape. Some who had pushed past the Strogoffs were already aflame; others caught fire as the burning fabric fell on them. Some just collapsed unburned. Some fell on the stairs just as they reached the Strogoffs; others made it past Ruth and Hyman, but then tumbled backward onto them.

> *"As the fire rushed up the stairway . . . it traveled . . . above the heads of persons ascending the stairway."*
>
> Boston Fire Department Report

The couple had gotten no further than the first step when Hyman fell. "He went down very heavy on my right arm," said Ruth. She grasped the banister with her left hand and pulled with all her might, but she could drag Hyman up only one more step. By now he was wedged under a heap of collapsed bodies and pressed into the stairs by the feet of others scrambling past.

James Lane may have been one of those who stepped on Hyman. Lane had lost track of Lauer after Lauer tried to cut down the satin ceiling, and there was no time to think about his friend. Starting up the stairs, but finding it blocked by bodies,

Lane saved himself by jumping on the banister and pulling himself over the human pile to the top. He didn't see Lauer anywhere at that moment and would never see him alive again.

Now the tops of the faux-cane walls lining the staircase were burning as the fire raced ahead of Ruth, who was still pulling at her husband in her desperation to wrench him free of the tangle of bodies at the foot of the stairs. Flames and the choking smoke enveloped Ruth. Her hat and jacket were burning, and Hyman's hand slipped from her grip. She crawled forward, making it to the top, and rolled around on the floor to extinguish the flames on her clothing. As she looked back, Ruth thought that she could barely make out her husband through the smoke. He lay there, still, partially covered by other bodies. He was most likely dead. She knew she couldn't help him, even though he was no more than 10 or 12 feet away. Further trying to rescue Hyman in the slender hope that he was still alive would have only assured that both of them would die.

She stood up, pulled the remnant of her jacket over her head, scrambled past the locked emergency exit door, and retraced the long U-turn to the revolving door out to the safety and fresh air of Piedmont Street, thinking through it all, "Hyman never said a word."

Ruth Strogoff may well have been the first person in the Cocoanut Grove to experience that stark instant of having to make the awful choice of turning away from a loved one in order to save one's self. Almost half of the people in the Grove would die that night, and many of the survivors would soon confront Ruth's choice of whether to save themselves or make a brave but futile effort to rescue a doomed spouse, friend, sibling, or sweetheart.

The sizzling fire and its shroud of thick smoke were now moving onto the main floor, where there were seven to eight hundred unsuspecting customers and employees. In another moment they would be hurtling into each other in a desperate search for the exits—and escape from the firetrap that the Cocoanut Grove had become.

CHAPTER 3

No Exit

This is no place for us.

———————————

Cocoanut Grove patron
Charles W. Disbrow Jr. to his wife, Peggy

NOT MUCH WIDER THAN an alley and otherwise nonde-
script, Piedmont Street was distinguishable only by the
vertical neon sign and the illuminated marquee that spanned the
top of the three arches at the entranceway to number 17. The
marquee's streamlined art deco letters announced that this was
the main entrance to Boston's famous Cocoanut Grove.

But behind this neat façade lay disorder. By November 28,
1942, the Grove had become an agglomeration of six buildings,
bounded on the south by Piedmont Street, on the north by the
equally narrow Shawmut Street, and on the east by Broadway.
As the club prospered, Barney had renovated the Grove from
the inside out without regard to the footprints of the original six
structures. The result was that behind the grand entranceway
there lay a confusing maze of public rooms, dressing rooms,
staircases, utility rooms, and corridors.

It is a maxim among fire code professionals that, unless directed
otherwise, a panicked crowd will try to leave the same way it came

in. Most of the Grove patrons had come in through the main-floor revolving door on the Piedmont Street side of the building.

The average customer desperate to escape the Grove would have known only two means of egress. The only public entries—and escape routes—from this approximately 10,000 square feet of public space were the revolving door at the main entrance at 17 Piedmont Street and the New Broadway Lounge doorway around the corner on Broadway. These two exits were nearly a full city block distant from one other, and each of them, in their own way, was lethal. (The first page of the illustrations section shows the various Grove exits described here.)

The revolving door (Exit #1) at the main entrance to 17 Piedmont Street brought patrons into the foyer area. Revolving doors, which were invented to control air exchange between the outside and inside of buildings, work well to control the orderly flow of traffic into a room, but a desperate crowd seeking to get out in a hurry easily jams them.

The second public exit (Exit #2), from New Broadway Lounge, was a single door that opened to a small vestibule from which customers went through a set of two more doors to get to Broadway. The interior door swung *into* the room. Doors that swing into public rooms are dangerous because they defy the flow of human traffic. A panicked crowd pressing against an inward-swinging door will seal itself within a burning building.

In addition to these two publicly known doors, there were seven other doors, generally familiar only to employees, making nine total possible doorway exits.

One of the nine possible exits (Exit #3) was in the basement. It could be reached by passing through a door in the back wall of the Melody Lounge, into a passageway, and then up three steps to a door with a wooden bar across it. This hidden exit led to a blind alley between the back of the Grove and an adjoining apartment building. A sewer pipe restricted the door so that it could only be opened—again, inward—18 inches. This door proved useless, but not because of its absurd dimensions. This was the door that John Bradley recalled too late—the one not far from the Melody Lounge's hard-to-locate kitchen door that "nobody thought about" dur-ing the panic. No one escaped through this door.

Then there was the door that Ruth Strogoff ran past on her long run to the revolving door. This door (Exit #4) was located at the top of the fifteen-step staircase to the Melody Lounge, and it could have pro-vided a quick exit for the

> *"Flame appeared at the street floor . . . within two to four minutes after it was first seen in the basement room. . . . A large and extremely hot volume of burning material, largely gaseous in form, appeared at the top of the stairway."*
>
> Boston Fire Department Report

Melody Lounge customers. It was equipped with a "panic lock," a lock that unlatched when the bar across the door was pressed. But the panic lock was rendered useless by an additional key lock. Over this door (today it seems a cruel taunt) was an illumi-nated EXIT sign.

Barney Welansky had made a simple business decision about all of the emergency doors. They were kept locked or obscured to discourage deadbeats from skipping on their checks. No in-spector from the City of Boston had ever challenged him on this practice.

Unlike the Strogoffs and the others who had remained down-stairs, Nathan Greer and Kathleen O' Neil had left just seconds before the danger was generally perceived (about 10:18 P.M.), and they made it upstairs unscathed. Nathan had lost track of Jim Jenkins on the stairs. Once upstairs, instead of making for the revolving door, Kathleen ran in the opposite direction toward the back of the foyer. She wanted to get her coat and fetch Ann McCardle from the ladies' room. Kathleen "was taking her time," said Nathan.

Then Nathan saw the fire ripping through the staircase corridor and starting to lick into the foyer. "Like a wind it swept up the stairs and I don't know why it moved so fast. It looked like a ball of fire traveling through the air," Nathan reported later. He opened the ladies' room door and shouted, "Get the hell out, there's a fire." He dragged Kathleen out and pulled her across the foyer to the revolving door. But the door was seized shut by the panicked crowd, with people's arms, legs, and shoulders jammed between the edges of the glass leaves and the frame.

Coast Guardsman Raymond N. Carter and his party had moved to the main floor before the fire because the Melody Lounge was so crowded. "All the tables and chairs were full," he reported later, but the situation was no better upstairs. "The tables up there were so close together we had to twist and turn to get to the dance floor," Carter said. When he saw the fire, he attempted to leave the building by the revolving door but saw that "people were piling up against the door."

Trapped inside by the jammed revolving door were Wilbur Sheffield and Charles Begotti, two of a party of thirteen men from the local General Electric plant. Sheffield had just pushed through the door and was standing inside the foyer when he heard the shouts of "FIRE." He turned to leave and started pushing against the exit side of the door, but it wouldn't budge. He looked over and saw his friend Begotti trapped between two panels on the entrance side. Begotti had been on his way in, but he saw the fire and turned to make the impossible effort of pushing the panel backward in the direction of the street.

When Nathan and Kathleen reached the frozen door, Nathan saw a woman aflame between two panels. She twisted, screamed, and fell dead, further blocking the door. "I hit it with all my might but it stuck," he said. Describing Sheffield and Begotti's counterproductive efforts to push the door in both directions at once, Nathan said, "People were pushing on both sides."

Sigmund Cohen, who had stepped out earlier for a cigarette, looked on helplessly. "People trying to force their way through the revolving door jammed the way. . . . There was nothing I could do but look on."

Finally, the door buckled under the superhuman force that a panicked crowd is capable of generating, and it crashed forward. Nathan jumped forward into the street, losing Kathleen's hand and his wristwatch as he went. Sheffield and Begotti also jumped forward to safety. But the fire followed in a voracious ball, hungry for the fresh supply of oxygen from Piedmont Street. "Everybody behind me was consumed, and Kathleen was right behind me," said Nathan.

At about the same moment Coast Guardsman Raymond Carter, who had been at the revolving door but had retreated because "people were piling up" there, had climbed onto the bar that ran along the Piedmont Street wall opposite the main Caricature Bar. Carter knew that there was a concealed window high above this bar. "You wouldn't know it was a window but I had seen it before," he reported later. He was looking for something to break the window when a blast of heat hit him. "I went out through the window," he said.

A friend of Wilbur Sheffield and Charles Begotti, Elisha Cobb, had the misfortune of entering just seconds before Sheffield had, and he was too far into the foyer to make an escape. He died from internal and external burns.

Ann McCardle, whose safety had caused Kathleen O'Neil to hesitate before leaving the building, had managed to climb through the ladies' room window to Shawmut Street. Hours later, Nathan learned that Kathleen's body was among those laid out in the garage of Waterman's Funeral Home. "When they found my girl's body, she had my wristwatch in her hand," said Nathan. Jim Jenkins's body was also at Waterman's garage.

Like Nathan and Kathleen, Joyce Spector had decided to go upstairs in those last critical seconds before the "little fire" consumed the Melody Lounge ceiling. Then she hesitated before retrieving her coat. "I thought of the girls in the ladies' room. So I put my head in the door and said, 'Hey girls, don't get excited, but there's a little fire downstairs and you'd better start getting out,'" she reported.

Her good deed done, Joyce started back for her coat. "But in that minute I had been in the ladies' room, the panic had got started. The whole place was one mob, shouting, screaming, pushing. There was smoke everywhere, and flames were shooting up the stairs where I had just come."

Joyce saw a woman knocked down by the crowd. The woman reached her hand up for help, but no one offered assistance. "The men were the worst. Honest. There were men pushing and hitting and shoving to get out." Joyce reached out for the woman. "Just then a big man pushed me in the back and knocked me down before I could get her hand."

Joyce started crawling—where to, she didn't know. There was too much smoke and heat for her to stand. Her eyes were useless in the blinding smoke, but she was saved by other senses. Joyce was "being pushed by feet trampling around me" when she felt a burst of fresh air.

The air was coming from another of the nine exits (Exit #5). At the center of the Shawmut Street wall of the main-floor dining room and below an EXIT sign were two wood slat "Venetian" doors that swung into the room to reveal another pair of doors in the exterior wall. Each of these exterior double doors was about 20 inches wide; they, too, were equipped with panic locks. However, the right-hand door was bolted shut at its top. On the night of the fire, as on other busy nights, extra tables and chairs blocked the cosmetic Venetian doors.

Joyce followed the trail of fresh air on her hands and knees to the double doors. Waiter Frank Accursio had opened one of these doors just seconds before, creating a meager 20-inch wide escape route. No one seemed to know about (or could see) the bolt that sealed the second 20-inch door.

Someone standing just outside the door grabbed Joyce's hand, "threw me across the sidewalk, and grabbed for more people inside." Joyce landed in the gutter. "It seemed like an hour I lay there. I couldn't tell. More people were pulled out and tossed down beside me." Then Joyce saw "that nice little man" who had been celebrating his silver wedding anniversary with his wife. "He was all cut up by glass or something. I guess he was dead."

Dead, too, was Joyce's fiancé, Justin Morgan, who was scheduled to enter the Navy on Monday morning. His body was recovered from Waterman's garage.

Joyce's skirt had been burned off and her long curly hair singed. After what she had gone through, Joyce would later think it odd that she still had her leopardskin hand warmer, or "muff." Even while being knocked down and trampled and crawling on her hands and knees, and then being thrown through the door to the safety of the gutter, she never let go of the muff.

> *"The fire passed thence through a connecting corridor into the Foyer."*
>
> Boston Fire Department Report

The superheated gas that appeared at the top of the "chimney" formed by the steep staircase from the Melody Lounge had now propelled itself around the U-turn into the foyer. The foyer was a 40-by-12-foot room with arched ceilings. Its walls were covered with artificial leather trimmed with rattan and lined with upholstered chairs.

The foyer's relatively open space and its flammable appointments provided the fire with a re-infusion of two essential elements, oxygen and fuel. Nearly all of the survivors who saw the fire enter the foyer from the basement used the same innocuous-sounding word to describe the effect of the fire at the top of the staircase—"poof." This "poof" was the silent explosion of the very hot but only partially burned carbon monoxide gas from the Melody Lounge finding the fresh air and abundant fuel of the foyer.

It was in the foyer where, on most nights, the elegant Angelo Lippi would control traffic. Except for brief interludes at other first-rate nightspots, Lippi had presided over the front of the house since the Grove's creation in 1927. His genial face crowned by pomaded hair and accented by a carefully trimmed handlebar mustache, Angelo—the "Count"—had been the face of the Grove's hospitality for fifteen years. Always impeccably attired in his tuxedo, he nightly implemented Barney Welansky's simple instructions: "Receive guests, see they were made comfortable, see that they left happy and see that they come back again."

However, on this night, as on most nights over the previous two months, Angelo was confined to his home with arthritis and gout. His assistant, the more plebeian headwaiter, Frank Balzarini, was doing his best to fill in, but he wasn't happy about his new role. In fact, that very afternoon Frank had visited Angelo at home to confide that he was soon leaving the job at the Grove to go to work in a munitions factory.

Although Frank was doing as well as he could, this Saturday night had become particularly stressful. Extra tables and chairs had been placed on every available inch of floor space, including a few in the passageway to the New Broadway Lounge. But even with the extra places, Frank had begun turning people away at nine o'clock, and he had borne the brunt of their disappointment.

It must have passed through Frank's mind that he should have started his job at the munitions factory weeks ago. He would be making more money with less stress. Whatever regrets he harbored about the timing of his decision to leave, Frank had to be buoyed by the idea that in a short while his circumstances would improve. He had no reason to believe otherwise, for until about 10:18 P.M., the thirty-seven-year-old Frank Balzarini could not have imagined that this was the last night of his life.

"Run like hell. Open up that Shawmut Street door," Balzarini screamed to waiter Frank Accursio, just about the same time that Nathan Greer, Katherine O'Neil, and Joyce Spector had seen the ball of flame and black smoke pushing up into the foyer. After the first shouts of FIRE, Balzarini had instructed wine steward Jacob Goldfine to get to the revolving door to supervise an orderly withdrawal.

Next to the revolving door was another possible means of egress (Exit #6). This was a conventional door to the right of the revolving doors, swinging inward and visible from the inside on this night only to the main-floor checkroom girls, Barbara O'Brien and Anne Lentini. This was because this door could be reached only by making one's way through the makeshift, lean-to checkroom that had been cobbled around it. As was the usual practice, this emergency door was locked on the night of November 28. In any event, it was further disguised and barricaded on the inside by the temporary wooden coatrack that hung across it on busy nights. No one escaped through this door. Anne Lentini, her hair aflame, escaped the fire, but even she didn't use this door. She ran out through the revolving door. Barbara O'Brien burned to death in the checkroom.

"I went to the revolving door and put my hand on the cable that opens it up," said Goldfine. That cable at the bottom of the door could have unfastened the glass partitions, allowing them to swing freely and create 58 1/2 inches—nearly 5 feet—of unobstructed egress.

"Someone stepped on my hand and I couldn't do anything. There were so many people around the door nobody could get out," Goldfine said later. He tried to make his way to the Venetian doors across the dining room, about 100 feet away from the fire, "but somebody threw a table at me. . . . I crawled underneath the legs of people." (It would have been just after this time that Nathan Greer, Wilbur Sheffield, Charles Begotti, and a few lucky others would have been falling with the collapsing revolving door panel into Piedmont Street.) As Goldfine got near the

Venetian doors on the Shawmut Street side of the dining room, he encountered Frank Balzarini shouting to the panicked crowd to move toward those doors and away from the fire that was rolling overhead from the foyer.

Frank Accursio had run ahead to the Venetian doors as instructed by Balzarini. With the crowd pressing on his back, he threw aside the tables and chairs blocking the decorative doors, pulled them apart and pressed against the panic bars of the metal double exit doors. The left door, 20 inches wide, yielded; the right wouldn't budge, held in place by a bolt at the top of the door that slid into a hole in the casing. Accursio, unfamiliar with this exit, couldn't see the bolt through the smoke. He pressed against the obstinate door, but the unseen bolt held. Another waiter, Daniel Joseph Rizzo, and a sailor picked up a table by its legs and hammered away to no avail. Accursio pressed and kicked at the right side until he, Rizzo, and the sailor were pushed through the open side by the throng that had been herded there by Balzarini. The momentum of the stampede also carried Balzarini and Goldfine through the open door.

Goldfine later reported, "I got out, went home, changed my clothes, and returned." As for Balzarini, two days later the *Boston Herald* reported, "Forced to the street by the crowd that rushed through ... Balzarini, 37, of Connecticut Avenue, East Natick, pushed his way through the crowd into the burning

> *"Thence the fire proceeded the length of the Foyer past the main entrance to the premises and traversed the length of the area containing the Caricature Bar. . . . As it traveled through the lobby toward the Caricature Bar, it was soon followed by a thick cloud of smoke."*
>
> Boston Fire Department Report

building and rescued a half a dozen unconscious women before he himself was killed."

At 10:19 P.M. Charles W. Disbrow Jr. told his wife, Peggy, with remarkably cool understatement, "This is no place for us." Disbrow and his wife, part of a party of nine, sat at a table near the center of the dining room, close to the crowded dance floor. They had just finished dinner and were waiting for the floor show to begin. Looking around idly, Disbrow noticed that, one after another, heads were turning toward the foyer and the bar. Then he sensed a building commotion at the Caricature Bar. "At first I thought some celebrators had started a fight." He realized very quickly that there was no fight. Disbrow saw a man jump onto the bar. "Two belches of flame seemed to be chasing him," he said.

The Caricature Bar was on the right side as one entered the Foyer from the revolving door entrance on Piedmont Street. The bar area was raised about 1 1/2 feet above the floor to facilitate viewing of the floor show in the adjoining main room, from which the bar area was separated only by a railing. The oblong bar was 48 feet long, reputed to be the largest in Boston, and surrounded by fixed chrome stools with seats covered in red leatherette. The whole bar area, in fact, was encased in red leatherette—the walls, ceiling, and the padded face of the bar itself. Photographs taken by Lynn Andrews, the Grove's photographer, and portraits of the regular patrons and famous visitors hung on the walls. Another bar ran along the Piedmont Street wall. Above this bar were four sealed casement windows, covered by dark curtains, with bottom sills 5 feet above the floor.

A large exhaust fan at the far end ventilated the bar area. It sucked the fire into the bar.

"I knew there would be a panic, and people had already started running away from the space near the bar," said Disbrow later.

Charles quickly decided that he and Peggy would find their own way to safety. They would not join the hundreds who would be pushing into the foyer in the direction of the revolving doors—and toward fire. Instead, the couple ran down the service stairs to the basement kitchen behind the Melody Lounge.

Then Disbrow thought that perhaps they had made a mistake. He and Peggy found about fifty frightened people in the kitchen searching for an exit in unfamiliar surroundings. "There was no smoke in the cellar as we entered. There seemed to be a line of people down there, about two abreast, and they were going toward a dark corner," he said. In that dark corner was a door to the refrigerator room that appeared to be a dead end. "We can't get out this way," someone screamed. Then the lights failed.

The Disbrows tried to return to the main floor, but by this time, everything—the basement, the staircase, and the main floor—was enveloped in blinding and choking smoke. The Disbrows and another couple decided against going back upstairs. "The smoke really saved us," Disbrow reported. They would take their chances on finding an escape route from the basement.

The foursome left the larger group, which was now enveloped by both smoke and panic. Their eyesight was useless in the black smoke, and they groped their way around the kitchen. "I didn't think we'd get out. We followed so many false trails down there," he said. Then Disbrow sensed a shaft of chilly November air pushing through the smoke. Following the current, he found a small boarded-up window high above the kitchen

service bar, just next to the door connecting to the Melody
Lounge. (This was the "invisible" door on the back wall of the
Melody Lounge through which Stanley Tomaszewski had led
Bill Connery.)

Disbrow jumped on the service bar and kicked away glasses
and bottles. He pulled away the boards and smashed his hand
through the remaining shards of glass. Two pipes ran across the
window so that there was only about 1 1/2 feet of vertical clear-
ance. He pulled Peggy up onto the bar and boosted her through
the narrow opening. Then he and the other man attempted to
boost the other woman through the window, but she lost her
footing and slid along the wall into the space between the back of
the service bar and the wall. They pulled her up and saw that her
face was cut. They managed to boost her up and through the
window; then Disbrow and the other man made their escapes.

Outside, the two couples found themselves in the blind alley
between the back of the club and a neighboring apartment building, the same alley that the forgotten door obstructed by the
sewer pipe opened to. They opened the alley door of the adjoining apartment building and confronted a very surprised Mrs.
Margaret Foley standing in the hallway. Unaware of the emergency next door, Mrs. Foley looked "as if she thought we were
crazy," said Disbrow. Put off by this disheveled bunch, Mrs.
Foley announced sternly, "You can't go through my house."

Disbrow was in no mood to explain. "'You bet we're going
through,' I said, and we tore through."

Mrs. Foley later estimated that, minutes after the Disbrows
had come through, as many as fifty people filed through her
hallway or through the adjoining alleyway to the street. Since

the only other way to Mrs. Foley's would have been through the door that no one remembered (Exit #3), the one blocked by a sewer pipe, it is certain that Charles W. Disbrow Jr. discovered one of the most effective emergency exits from the Grove, a 1 1/2-by-2-foot space about 7 or 8 feet above the basement floor.

After losing control of the fire in the palm tree, John Bradley retreated to the kitchen. There he found several employees, including Mrs. Catherine Swett, the head cashier. Mrs. Swett sat at her desk, clutching the bulky cash box that held all of the night's receipts for the entire club. Bradley told Mrs. Swett and the others to get out and then returned to the Melody Lounge to make another attempt to control the fire and panic.

Henry Bimler, a waiter in the main room, ran down the service stairs to the kitchen. "I asked Catherine Swett to give me her cash box and get out," said Bimler. "She kept saying she couldn't leave the money. I said it was dangerous, but she wouldn't go."

Meanwhile, John Bradley had quickly assessed the situation in the Melody Lounge and decided that there was nothing he could do. He returned to the kitchen, but he could see nothing through the blinding smoke that now filled the room. "I called, 'Anybody there?' There was no answer," said Bradley. He then climbed onto the service bar and pulled his portly frame through the same little window that Charles Disbrow's group had.

Several hours later, when the initial list of the dead was compiled, Catherine Swett's name was on it. The next day the *Boston*

Herald would carry a small story about Catherine Swett headlined "Loyal to the End."

Donald Jeffers and his wife, Mildred, who had watched "everyone laughing and joking" as the Grove employees danced around that "little blaze," realized that they were in mortal danger. The little blaze had become a blue and orange—or yellow—flash across the ceiling of the room and had engulfed it in thick, caustic smoke. Seeing the flames rushing past and over the crowd in the public staircase, the Jefferses made their way in the opposite direction, through the door on the back wall of the Melody Lounge and into the kitchen, the same route that Stanley Tomaszewski had taken with Ensign Bill Connery.

There was no relief in the kitchen from the smoke, and the Jeffers were immediately separated in the blackness. Unable to hear Don's response to her calls to him, Mildred groped around and soon discovered that window over the service bar—the Disbrows' escape route. Then Mildred made the same sad choice that Ruth Strogoff had made moments earlier, to save herself. She climbed on the service bar, went through the window, and then made her way to the street through Mrs. Foley's now well-traveled hallway. Mildred then suffered an hour of guilt and anxiety walking around the Grove countless times, searching the piles of bodies now being laid on the sidewalks by policemen, firemen, civil defense workers, and passersby.

After losing track of Mildred in the dark smoke, Don Jeffers crawled on the floor of the kitchen, searching for his own escape. "A man yelled to me from the darkness saying, 'This is the refrigerator. Jump in quick. It's fire proof.'" Jeffers opened the door to the walk-in box and joined two men and two women.

"Several times we opened the door and heard the most terrifying screams and shrieks. One of the women with us prayed more fervently than I ever heard from the pulpit," he said. After about a half hour, the group heard the sounds of splashing water and pushed at the door tentatively to shout for help. A fireman responded and came to the refrigerator. It was still impossible to see, and the fireman instructed them to take hold of the fire hose and follow it to the street. Once on the street, Don replicated the same desperate circles around the block that Mildred had begun as soon as she had made her escape.

At about 11:30 P.M., more than one hour after Mildred had climbed through the window, the Jefferses' grisly search for each other among the piles of the dead and dying ended. They were reunited on the street.

CHAPTER 4

The Eight-Minute Fire

It was just a wild outburst of everybody rushing and swinging their arms and fighting and hollering and screaming. . . . It was like a lot of wild animals pushing people around.

Cocoanut Grove patron Harry Thomas

From [the bar] or from the Foyer itself, the fire spread to the main dining room.

Boston Fire Department Report

B Y 10:20 P.M. AT THE LATEST, as if to advise the patrons that there would be no escape from its authority, the fire was marching into the main dining room from two separate flanks. Feeding on the fresh fuel of the foyer's trappings and then sucked into the Caricature Bar by the exhaust fan, it was now converging from both those areas into the main-floor dining room, hungry for more oxygen and fuel.

The main-floor dining room was the largest single area open to the public, a 60-by-60-foot square room, and the Grove's showplace. In the center of the room was a 600-square-foot wooden dance floor, surrounded by tables and chairs. The six "palm trees"—actually structural columns—provided the signature décor of the Grove: three on each side of the dance floor.

A patron entering the main dining room from the foyer would see the orchestra platform at the far end of the room about 4 feet above the floor. Under the orchestra area rested a sliding platform that was pulled out over the dance floor for the floorshows.

To the right of the orchestra platform, as patrons came in from the foyer, was the opening to the L-shaped, orange velour-covered passageway to the New Broadway Lounge. Extra tables and chairs had been set up in that opening to accommodate the overflow crowd.

On the left side of the orchestra platform was another door that opened, inward, to Shawmut Street. This "service door" (Exit #7) was always locked when the club was open for business. The key to this lock was kept in the basement kitchen. Further to the east along Shawmut Street were two doors that were of no help to the fire's victims. One of these (Exit #8) was a locked, inward-swinging door hidden behind a warren of dressing and utility rooms. The other door (Exit #9) was also locked and inward swinging. Welansky had submitted plans to the building department that showed that Exit #9 was to be freely accessible to New Broadway Lounge patrons in an emergency. Instead, he built a checkroom that completely blocked it.

The Shawmut Street side of the dining room was a false wood veneer wall hiding three large plate-glass windows. Had the panels not obscured them, these large windows might have provided an escape route for hundreds of people.

Extending about 8 feet from this wall was a Spanish tile canopy, and the floor area under it was raised about 6 inches above the main floor. This area and a similar tile canopy and platform on the opposite side backing up to the Caricature Bar area were referred to as the "arcades."

Against the wall opposite the orchestra platform, immediately to the left as one entered from the foyer, was the "terrace." Built about 2 feet above the floor, the terrace was the club's VIP area, and it provided a commanding view of the grand main dining room. The terrace was reached by a short staircase at its center and was surrounded on three sides by a wrought-iron railing.

Over the dance floor was a 900-square-foot rolling roof that Barney Welansky had installed in 1934, shortly after he had inherited the Grove. During mild weather, he opened the roof to allow dancing under the stars. When not in use, as was the case in November, the rolling roof was closed and concealed from below by billowy blue satin fabric. The celestial blue effect extended from wall to wall. All told, the main dining room had about 3,600 square feet of fabric ceiling. In addition, the orchestra platform was decorated with the same fabric on its walls and ceiling, except that it was the color of "mirage satin egg." The orchestra platform also had a fabric stage curtain across the front.

The dining room was a tightly enclosed tinderbox.

On November 28 a party of twelve sat in the Shawmut Street arcade, including John C. Gill, Boston College's alumni secretary, and his wife, Margaret. Despite BC's crushing defeat at the hands of the Holy Cross squad that afternoon, John and Margaret had decided to attend a long-planned Saturday night victory party at the Grove. This was a Thanksgiving weekend tradition. Why miss the fun just because your team lost by six touchdowns? Besides, the party was hosted by an important person, John Walsh, chairman of the Boston Committee for Public Safety, a wartime mobilization-planning agency. As it turned out, his organization was sorely tested that evening.

Everyone was waiting for the start of the show, which was to be signaled by the tenor Billy Payne's rendition of "The Star Spangled Banner," a nightly practice since the beginning of the war. The Gills sat at the far end of the table, with their backs to the foyer. The back-up band was playing, and the dance floor was jammed. They were surrounded by the loud sounds of conversation and laughter coming from other tables, the dance floor, and the bar.

Then John Gill gradually became aware of an unsettling sound, which he described as "a vague flurry," mixing with the sounds of merriment. In an instant, this flurry mushroomed into the sounds of a building panic—crashing tables and breaking bottles, glasses, and dinnerware. Turning in their chairs, the Gills were stunned to see a tongue of flame roll along the ceiling, barely touching the flimsy fabric material. Then came the screams of "FIRE" as balls of flame fell upon tables, the bar, and the bandstand and began to move down the walls. The floor rumbled with the vibration of stampeding feet.

"Keep calm. It's a fire. Keep calm. It's a fire," he repeatedly told those rushing around him. No one heeded his sensible advice. Then he saw Margaret pushed to the floor by the crowd clamoring to avoid the falling fireballs and searching for the exit doors. As he moved to help her, the panicked customers rushing past bounced John from side to side. Then he fell, his body covering Margaret. He scrambled to his feet and tried to get Margaret to hers, but they were knocked down repeatedly, climbed over and stepped on by the wild crowd. He felt feet on his back and neck and thought, "They're going over us. They're going over us to freedom!" In fact, for most, there was no freedom— just chaos.

By now, the room had darkened, either from the burning of electrical wiring or by the density of the smoke—or both. Nevertheless, there were flashes of illumination from the fire, and John could see his fellow patrons, many with their clothes afire and women with their long hair aflame, beating themselves to extinguish the flames while running haphazardly in every direction to avoid the fluttering sheets of burning fabric falling everywhere.

The flames had not touched John, but the superheated air had singed his hair, and the skin on his face was peeling. The time to reason with the crowd had passed; it was time for the Gills to save themselves. John got to his feet and pulled Margaret to hers. With one arm around his wife, he used the other to make his way through the frantic men and women whose stampede threatened to throw them back to the floor. John and Margaret made it to one of the Shawmut Street doors, the half of the double doors that waiter Frank Accursio had opened. John recalled later: "I don't remember that we were borne through that little door, but we must have been. I don't know whether we were shoved through standing up or whether we crawled."

The Gills' journey from their table through that "little door" took seconds, no more than a minute. Margaret, having been shielded by John's body, was bruised but not burned. John's burns were superficial, and the couple was treated at Boston

City Hospital and released after a short stay. They were among the lucky ones.

Most of the dining room terrace had been taken up by a party of about thirty people hosted by New England movie distributors and theater executives to honor cowboy movie star Charles "Buck" Jones. Now a forgotten name, Buck Jones had been a superstar in the '30s. Beginning in silent movies, Jones had successfully made the transition to talkies; in 1936, he was voted the country's favorite Western movie hero. By 1942, he had starred in more than two hundred movies and serials. Boston was the final leg of an exhausting cross-country tour that Jones had begun weeks earlier in California—a combination of war-bond rallies and promotions for his *Rough Rider* series, in which he co-starred with another cowboy movie legend of the time, "Colonel" Tim McCoy.

Buck was especially popular with children. He said that he never played the villain because "the little shavers wouldn't like it." That morning a crowd of 12,000 little shavers and their parents had been in the Boston Garden for a mass meeting of the Buck Jones fan club, where Buck entreated kids and parents to buy war stamps and bonds. Then Buck had gone to the children's hospital to cheer up some young patients. There photographers took pictures of him in a gray ten-gallon hat, smiling down at little Georgie Piette, a very sick four-year-old. That afternoon he sat in a drizzling rain in Fenway Park as the guest of honor in Mayor Tobin's box, watching Holy Cross trounce Boston College.

By the end of the afternoon, Buck was exhausted and suffering from a bad cold. He begged off his scheduled 9:30 appearance at a USO facility, the Buddies Club, and had tried to get out of the dinner planned in his honor. Marty Sheridan, a local newspaperman who was handling Buck's public relations in Boston, encouraged him not to miss the Grove affair. Realizing that the local movie executives were too important to snub, Buck reluctantly agreed to attend as planned.

The floor show had been scheduled to begin at 10:15, but "the girls were late coming down," Mickey Alpert, the Grove's entertainment coordinator, later recalled. Alpert caught up with his pal, singer Billy Payne, and said, "I'm tired Billy. Let's sit down." As usual, Alpert had spent the evening schmoozing and glad-handing the guests in the dining room. It was the same tiring ritual he went through every night; it came with the job. The delay in starting the show was a welcome breather.

But just as he and Billy sat down, someone on the terrace called for Mickey to come on up and meet Buck Jones. Alpert stood up and began to move toward the terrace steps when Billy Payne said, "Hey, Mickey, it's a fight." Like so many others, Payne had mistaken the excitement in the foyer and the shouts of FIRE to be the commotion of a "fight." Alpert turned to see the fire flashing through the foyer and coming directly at the terrace.

The terrace, just off the foyer, was the first section of the main room to be overwhelmed by flames and smoke. Until then, the party for Buck had been a happy gathering. It was largely composed of old friends and business acquaintances; some were sharing pictures of their children just before the fire reached them. But in an instant, all camaraderie was destroyed. Insurance executive Abe Yarchin remembered, "It was every man for himself." The frightened crowd—and the railing—trapped him and his wife, Goldie, on the terrace. "I don't remember anything except finding myself in the hospital," he said afterward.

Harry Thomas, the East Coast sales manager for Buck Jones's Monogram Pictures, recalled: "It was just a wild outburst of everybody rushing and swinging their arms and fighting and hollering and screaming. . . . It was like a lot of wild animals pushing people around." Thomas made it down from the terrace and then was knocked to the floor. Weakened by the fumes, he lay there in the dark under a pile of bodies.

> *"The great mass of compressed partially burned gases spread . . . into the Broadway Lounge."*
>
> Boston Fire Department Report

The décor of the New Broadway Lounge lacked the obvious tinder of the Melody Lounge and the main dining room, particularly their fabric ceilings. Nevertheless, after rampaging elsewhere through the club, the increased heat of the fire generated an intense pressure that pushed the flame and gases into the narrow passageway leading to the new room. Here was where the most complete burning occurred and where authorities found twenty-five incinerated bodies. The heat and pressure generated in the passageway created a virtual blowtorch pointed directly at the New Broadway Lounge.

Sitting together in the lounge had been Barney's brother, Jimmy Welansky, Suffolk County Assistant District Attorney Garret Byrne, and Captain Joseph A. Buccigross. Captain Buccigross headed the local police precinct that included the Grove and other top Boston clubs like the Mayfair and the Latin Quarter. When asked several days later why he had been at the Grove that Saturday night, Buccigross's stiff reply was that, despite being in civilian clothes, he was there "to see that order was maintained and to see that the licensees lived up to the letter of their license."

The reality was a great deal less official. Welansky, Byrne, and Buccigross sat at a table chatting amiably over drinks about a current murder case and about the New Broadway Lounge itself, which Buccigross hadn't seen before.

"Then a waitress came out of the dining room," reported the captain, "and said, 'Mr. Welansky, there's a fire in the main dining room.' Welansky left at once."

Because of its comparative remoteness from the main building, the crowd in the New Broadway Lounge was unaware for several minutes of the destruction being wrought next door. In those minutes, many of the patrons in the other rooms who were not yet taken down by burns or smoke saw the New Broadway Lounge as their last clear chance for escape. The crowd, numbering in the hundreds, rolled through the passageway and slammed into the 250 or so unprepared patrons sitting in the lounge. The heavy smoke, and then the fire, followed. The only way out for these several hundred people was through the 36-inch-wide, inward-swinging door to Broadway Street.

It could have been as late as 10:20 when Jimmy Welansky was informed by the waitress of the fire. "I got the smell of smoke," said Captain Buccigross, and then "the stampede came into the room." Buccigross and Assistant D.A. Byrne tried to calm the crowd, with little success. "They pushed me over a stool," said the captain. "But I got up and assisted in getting people out until flames came through." Buccigross and Byrne said the pressure of the panicked crowd eventually carried them through the doorway.

Joseph Kelly was one of the patrons who would soon be running through the passageway to the new lounge. He was at the

Caricature Bar just moments before the fire rolled through. He saw the fire just as it pushed up into the foyer, a distance of more than 60 feet from his bar stool. Then, the fire "lifted a little and spread" into the bar area and the main dining room "in a matter of instants," said Kelly. Fortunately, he was sitting next to the passageway to the New Broadway Lounge. As he ran through that corridor, Kelly realized that he was just steps ahead of a tunnel fire. "There seemed to be a natural draft . . . a current I guess . . . through the passageway and out that exit," he said. Then as he reached the end of the passageway, the flame flashed over his head and into the room. He ran toward the door "under the fire," he reported later.

Kelly had observed that the fire had been a ball of flame in the foyer, but in the New Broadway Lounge, "it had leveled out onto the ceiling and under it a heavy layer of smoke and gas." Kelly described how he bent over just enough to stay under the sheet of fire and smoke: "It got down to the six-foot level. . . . The fire and smoke were stratified. . . . There was a clear space under the smoke, and it was in that clear space that I managed to escape." He ran past people falling unconscious or dead to the floor and reached the door. It was jammed with "perhaps 50 or 100 people" scrambling to escape. He plunged in. "The crowd had a twisting motion," said Kelly. "I must have got caught in the vortex of it, or the center of that confusion, and been twisted out. I landed on Broadway, not of my own volition, feeling for a moment that I might be crushed when I was in the middle of the thing."

Harold Segool was standing on Broadway. He had just escaped from the burning new lounge with two of his three companions—his friend's wife would be found dead in the ladies' room. The three stood on the street and saw a man try to climb through a small opening in the glass block. The efforts of Deputy Chief Stickel's men to save him were fruitless. Segool and his friends watched in horror as the man burned to death, despite the fire hoses being played on him. "He was half in and half out," said Segool.

Cab driver Sam Meyers, a passerby, ran to the Broadway doors to help. He stepped into the little vestibule to assist people through, but a man who was "hollering and screeching" blocked the inner door. The man would not come out to the street, and he wouldn't let others pass. "Then a sailor hit him. . . . I found out he had stopped people from getting outside because he thought his wife was inside. I dragged him into the street. About 10 people got out," Meyers said, before the door became jammed again with the clawing crowd.

Soon after the fire had reached the new lounge, the lights went out. The darkness, together with the frenzied stampede from the main dining room, whipped the panic to an even higher level. When the lights failed, "everyone went crazy," said Louis Hern, who, with his wife, Susie, tried to make for the exit door ahead of the smoke and the terrified horde. "People knocked down chairs and tables in their haste to get out, only to trip over them as the crowd behind them pressed on," said Hern. He lost Susie's hand. "I was lifted off my feet and literally carried to the door," he reported. But he'd lost track of Susie, and then "I must have gone crazy," he said. Someone pulled Hern through the doors onto Broadway. Then, said Hern, "for what seemed like hours, I ran up and down the street shrieking, 'Susie, Susie.' Then I got back my senses and went back to the pile."

Hern systematically peeled bodies from the pile on the side-walk and saw a purple sleeve that looked like his wife's. "Thank God," he said later. "It was Susie, her face blackened; she'd been way down at the bottom. She told me later that she had given up all hope. She thought I was behind her and didn't care if she went, for she knew I'd gone too."

There was in Hern's account of having "gone crazy" a curious echo of Sam Meyers's description of the hysterical man who endangered himself and the others behind him when he blocked the door while "hollering and screeching" for his wife. But Louis Hern was a respectable, articulate, successful insurance executive, and one might assume that he would not fit the profile of hysterical, panic-stricken victim.

In fact, however, given the convergence of terrible circumstances, everyone fits the profile.

CHAPTER 5

Don't Panic

An individual in a crowd is a grain of sand amid other grains of sand, which the wind stirs up at will.

Gustave Le Bon,
La Psychologie des Foules
[The Psychology of Crowds] (1895)

"IF YOU ACT LIKE human beings, we'll all get out," Bernard Levin screamed at the top of his lungs to everyone around him in the main dining room, above all to his wife, her sister, her sister's husband, and two friends. But his five companions—hypnotized by panic—scattered in different directions, without reason. Maybe they were trampled; maybe they trampled others. Only Bernard made it out alive. A crowd in panic has no sense.

"It was like a lot of wild animals pushing people around," was Harry Thomas's description of the mob around the terrace that knocked all 250 pounds of him to the floor, where he was promptly trampled and then buried under a pile of other unfortunates who suffered the same shabby treatment. A crowd in panic has no sense *and* no conscience.

Sense and conscience are actually two sides of the same coin. "Right conduct is thought-out conduct. Conscience is a way of thinking things," said American social psychologist Edward Alsworth Ross, one of the pioneers of crowd studies at the turn of the twentieth century. According to Ross, the exercise of conscience in a crowd under stress consists of adherence to tested, thought-out rules of order—good sense. When a crowd member does unto others as he would have them do unto him, both sensible and decent results tend to ensue. Both the individual and the group are likely to be better off. Bernard Levin and Harry Thomas came to understand this point instinctively.

As it happened, Levin and Thomas, with their allusions to humans behaving like animals, struck on appropriate images to describe the contagion of unreasoning fear that infected the crowd at the Grove. Panic means—literally—human beings behaving like animals. The word is derived from "Pan," the mythological part-human, part-animal god of the forests and wild animals. Ugly and feral, Pan is the antithesis of the sublimely beautiful Apollo, god of the "civilized" qualities of culture and sophistication.

Like sublime beauty, the veneer of civilization can prove to be only skin-deep. When the forces of Pan grip a crowd, its members lose their tenuous hold on reason and conscience. At that point, differences in intellectual and moral attainments become meaningless. The college professor and the illiterate, the honorable and the corrupt, all become unthinking and selfish animals. These irrational tendencies—they could also be thought of as "uncivilized" or "immoral"—are always lurking under the surface and always poised to assert themselves. These dark proclivities are the only "common property" of the random crowd, wrote French social theorist Gustave Le Bon, another of the early students of crowd behavior.

A random crowd—a gathering not bound together by common interests such as family or community ties—is the lowest form of human association, and therefore the most easily panicked. The only common bond of a random crowd is the accident of its location. Like nightclub patrons everywhere, each Grove patron became a part of the crowd for what must have seemed to them, in retrospect, trifling reasons.

Joyce Spector and Justin Morgan had gone to the Grove on impulse, after their Saturday evening playing gin rummy together proved too tame. Another couple, Claudia Nadeau and John O'Neil, had a last-minute change of mind that led them to move their wedding celebration from the Latin Quarter to the Grove. Buck Jones, exhausted and sick, didn't want to be in the Grove at all but resigned himself to attending because of business imperatives. Ensign Bill Connery, far from his hometown of Dubuque, Iowa, and his roommate, Lieutenant David Fretchling, were chasing girls. In short, the crowd at the Grove was there because it was *the* place to go, which was not much of a bond at all.

Taken as a group, the Grove patrons shared no common goals, creed, or agreed-upon rules of conduct that might have determined how its members should behave when placed under stress. When faced with the terror of the fire, there was only one general code of conduct. As Abe Yarchin observed from the terrace, "It was every man for himself." Those in the crowd were, to paraphrase Le Bon, so many grains of sand that the winds of irrationality would stir up at will.

Random crowds are always on the verge of disorder. These groups, described by sociologists as "heterogeneous" crowds, are composed of strangers touching strangers, and such crowds have inherent physical tensions that predispose them to chaos—only the agitation of fear need be added. The crowd constricts one's personal space. As the physical press of the crowd limits the individual's voluntary movements, his or her ability to independently appraise a dangerous situation is constricted.

Edward Alsworth Ross, writing in 1908, described the deflation of ego that at one time or another everyone has experienced in a crowd. "The same pressure on the body that prevents voluntary movement," wrote Ross, "conveys promptly to him all the electrifying swayings and tremors that betray the emotions of the mass. The squeeze of the crowd tends to depress the self sense." Many of the Grove survivors later remarked about the difficulty—before the fire—of moving freely within the tangle of tables, around the dance floor, or along the bars. One complained, "We had to wriggle through the crowd to get to our table." These survivors realized, too late, that their fellow patrons were, as the expression goes, "too close for comfort."

Of course, not every assemblage degenerates into chaos. Large crowds collect without incident every day at theaters, sporting events, and political demonstrations. What was added to the mix at the Grove was a universal fixation, the generally perceived fear of the fire and the smoke, compounded by the fear that there was no escape.

The Grove patrons had very good reasons to be frightened. Those not killed immediately could barely breathe and were blinded by the acrid, coal-black smoke. Many had their skin peeling off their faces while they were stumbling over the dead and dying. Being frightened in these circumstances is a natural reaction.

Physically, this reaction is as old as human evolution. When faced with danger, the body prepares to fight or to flee. Of course, in the Grove there was no question of fighting—fleeing was the only alternative. This is not an inherently rational process. In threatening situations, the body's chemistry rules: metabolism speeds up, the heart races, the rate of breathing increases, muscles contract, vision may become blurred, the person may feel faint, the skin tingles, and the individual may not be able to control bowel or urinary functions. In evolutionary terms, the individual with the most highly developed "flight or fight" response had the best chance of surviving and, therefore, reproducing.

However, when such a response takes place in a crowd setting where the only choice is flight, the reasoning power of individual members is weakened. The hysterical man—perhaps it was even Louis Hern—who blocked the exit from the New Broadway Lounge because he had lost track of his wife, risked his own life and the lives of others behind him. One passerby recalled seeing a woman who tried repeatedly to get to the exit door, but each time she got close "somebody would pull her back in."

Le Bon's harsh judgment about such behavior was that "in crowds it is stupidity and not mother-wit that is accumulated." Ross made the same point more gently: "There is no question that, taken herdwise, people are less sane and sensible than they are dispersed."

In addition to these universal crowd tendencies, there was one unique behavioral factor at work at the Grove—alcohol.

While none of the autopsies of the victims were directed at determining whether they were debilitated by drink, it is certain that a number of the patrons had consumed more than a few highballs, Manhattans, and Cuba Libras by 10:15 P.M. The disorientating effects of even moderate amounts of alcohol, mixed with the terror of the fire, could only have increased the mental effort required to appraise the danger and plan a response to it.

The common images of panic as a force greater and more powerful than the members of the group are very telling. Crowds are described as being "gripped" or "engulfed" in a "wave" or "contagion" of panic. Unreasoning fear is transmitted among crowd members like a contagious disease. When a frightened individual in a panicked crowd looks about and observes that others share his or her terror, or that others are being taken down by the threat, the result is that the crowd determines the individual's signals for behavior. The panicky individual becomes credulous; he believes that the choices he observes the others making should be his choices too. He joins the stampeding herd or rushes about pointlessly, as though part of a frenzied pack of wild animals.

But the pack cannot plan, evaluate, or make informed choices, and the individual who surrenders his autonomy to the group is apt to make choices that harm not only his own interests but also those of the group as a whole. The effect of an excited crowd on the individual is akin to a mass hypnotic state, where planning functions are reduced and the subjects become highly suggestible.

Waiter Charles Mikalonis experienced just such a hypnotic spell. He had been standing directly in front of the revolving door, bidding some customers a good night, when the fire roared up the staircase from the Melody Lounge into the foyer. The customers immediately, and sensibly, pushed through the door to Piedmont Street, but Mikalonis, for reasons he could never explain, let the wild crowd in the foyer dictate his response to the danger. Rather than taking the few steps through the revolving door that would have brought him to the immediate safety of the street, he fell in with the frightened mob running across the dining room—a distance of well over 100 feet. He then scrambled up the stairs to the second-floor dressing room, excused himself to a naked showgirl, climbed through a window, and attempted to reach the roof. Not strong enough to pull himself up, Mikalonis dangled by his fingertips from the roof's edge until he fell to the street. When asked why he had increased the danger to himself for no good reason, Mikalonis could only offer a familiar explanation: "I felt weak and couldn't think. . . . I lost my sense right then and there."

Not everyone at the Grove was suggestible to the same degree. Certainly, Charles Disbrow Jr. was frightened and anxious when he quietly told his wife, Peggy, "This is no place for us," just before they separated from the crowd to find their own escape from danger. Terrified as he may have been, Disbrow acted autonomously, the signals for his behavior being internal and not dictated by the crowd. Behavior, even highly emotional behavior, that rationally reduces a threat, such as seeking an escape from a fire or avoiding a stampeding crowd, is not panic but the exercise of an individual's good sense.

In a panicked crowd, however, those who keep their heads will inevitably lose the battle. "Feelings, having more means of vivid expression, run through a crowd more easily than ideas," wrote Ross. What chance of success do even the simplest ideas—like "stay calm" or "don't panic"—have when most of the crowd is "fighting," "running," "hollering," "screaming," "screeching," and "stampeding"? John Gill's reward for keeping his head and entreating those around him to stay calm was to see his wife, Margaret, thrown to the floor just before he was heaped on top of her and trampled on by those barreling over them.

Tenor Billy Payne tried to calm one obviously frightened man in front of the terrace. "It can't be a big fire," said Payne, "it will be put out." "Put it out *nothing!*" was the man's response to Payne before he punched him in a frantic effort to escape.

All the evidence indicated that many in the Grove crowd resisted, sometimes violently, every effort to maintain order. Second Class Petty Officer Joseph Lawrence Lord witnessed firsthand evidence of such violence. While helping to pull the dead out of the Grove after the fire, Lord discovered a young naval lieutenant at the bottom of a pile of about a dozen bodies. "His arms were outstretched," said Lord, who concluded that the lieutenant had died while gesturing for calm. "He apparently was just beaten down by the crowd, pretty evenly divided between men and women." The sailor had "hardly a stitch of clothing on him," said Lord.

The number of people killed by panic at the Grove can never be known. Ironically, the frightened crowd may in fact have saved some, like Harry Thomas. Thrown to the floor and buried under piles of others, Thomas and some additional survivors may have been shielded from the flames and able to breathe the coolest, least befouled, and most oxygen-rich air left in the rooms. One serviceman saved himself by sitting in a corner and urinating on a napkin, which he placed over his nose and mouth as a barrier to the choking smoke. Little Anthony Marra, a fifteen-year-old bar boy, stuck his face into a large container of ice cream—reported to be maple walnut—to cool his burning face and give himself time to plan his escape.

Nevertheless, for every such story there were many Hyman Strogoffs, Kathleen O'Neils, and the nameless man who was burned to death "half in and half out" of the glass-block window of the New Broadway Lounge.

Crowd control comes down to the maintenance of order. Even a frightened crowd can be kept in good order if its members believe that there is an escape route. The panic at the Grove consisted of three elements. First was the universal propensity of all random crowds to degenerate into chaos. The second was the threat of the fire and smoke. In the face of the first two conditions alone, panic might have been kept to a minimum had it not been for the third element: the well-founded fear that there were very few exits and that there would be a deadly competition for the few that existed.

Crowds will always be inherently unstable, and accidents, like Stanley Tomaszewski's match on the palm tree, are ever-present risks. The advice "don't panic" is empty unless the individual believes that he will be rewarded for keeping his head. At the time of the fire, Robert Moulton was the highly professional technical secretary of the National Fire Protection Association (NFPA). In the report he authored for the NFPA two months after the fire, Moulton stated a succinct proposition: "As long as people are moving freely toward an assured place of safety, there is little danger of panic even though the fire may be rather close behind them." The strongest evidence in support of this statement is that the overwhelming majority of Grove employees escaped safely. Although they were frightened and they ran, they knew which way to run.

The search for answers to the question of why there was no "assured place of safety" for the Cocoanut Grove patrons on the night of November 28, 1942, would consume the City of Boston for months to come.

CHAPTER 6

The Unalterable Laws

I was at the door dragging them out, laying them on the
sidewalk wherever we could put them.

Fireman Dennis Sullivan

IT HAD TAKEN ONLY eight minutes. The records of the
Boston fire department show that Deputy Chief Stickel witnessed the doomed customer trying to crawl through the glass-
block window of the New Broadway Lounge at 10:23. By that
time, the fire that had begun at 10:15 in the cellar nearly a city
block away had climbed the steep staircase to the main floor,
dashed past the locked exit door, retraced the patrons' awkward
U-turn, run through the foyer and into the Caricature Bar,
overwhelmed the main dining room, and finally rolled through
the L-shaped corridor into the New Broadway Lounge, where
the terrified patrons raced each other to the one remaining
exit—the inward-swinging door onto Broadway.

Because it had moved with such astonishing speed, the fire's
energy was quickly spent. The main body of flame would be extinguished by 10:45, only thirty minutes after the "little" fire
had begun in the palm tree.

The firefighters' main problem was rescue. As the first contingents of firefighters arrived, most of the thousand occupants were still sealed inside. In those earliest minutes, the firemen would battle the heat and smoke and lingering flames, while trying to penetrate the building to reach trapped customers and employees. They would have the same difficulty getting into the Cocoanut Grove as the occupants had getting out.

Under streams of water from 18 hose lines played on all three sides of the Grove, the firemen carefully effected their preliminary entries into the buildings, becoming the first outside witnesses to the human toll. No training could have prepared them for what they saw. There were bodies everywhere.

Lieutenant Myles Vincent Murphy was one of the first to enter the vestibule to the New Broadway Lounge. After having been pushed into the street by the smoke and heat, the hosemen counterattacked and reached the entryway. Now Murphy's problem was to snake the line of hose inside, first through the double doors on the street and then through the inward-swinging interior door. "Our object was to knock the fire down in order to keep it away from the people who were trapped," Murphy recalled. But the bodies blocked the inward-swinging door. "They were piled high," the lieutenant said. "You couldn't get in there. We had to crawl over their bodies to get in there. . . . I would say we removed about thirty people."

Deputy Chief John McDonough, who was supervising the entry on the Piedmont Street side, discovered the locked emergency door at the top of the Melody Lounge staircase. His men smashed this door open with axes but were initially pushed back by what he described as a "frightful" blast of heat. Oddly, though, there was little or no flame, said McDonough. A fire-

man then crawled in and shouted back, "There are a lot of bodies here." McDonough recalled, "The bodies were wedged in
pretty well. The firemen would go in and reach a pair of legs,
hold on, and I would have different members pull him out by
the legs."

At that moment, patron Thomas Sheehan Jr. was trapped at
the bottom of the Melody Lounge staircase behind the pile of
bodies being unraveled by the firemen. "There was a pile of
people four or five deep at the door," said Sheehan. Most were
dead, but some were alive, "wriggling and shouting," he said.
"Men were calling women's names but I don't remember any of
them. I couldn't see any other way out." Sheehan could feel the
skin on his face peeling. "Then I ran and dove right over the
pile and landed on my head," he said. "I don't know how they
got there so quickly, but I was surprised to see two firemen outside the door grabbing arms and hauling people out of the pile."

On the opposite side of the club, ladderman James McNeil
may have been the first to enter through the Shawmut Street
double doors that had only minutes earlier been obscured and
blocked by tables, chairs, and Venetian doors. McNeil and other
firemen smashed open the right-hand door that had been bolted
shut. He then dropped to his hands and knees and crawled in a
few feet, where he found a tangle of "twenty to twenty-five bodies. . . . Some of them were moving. . . . You would see a head
moving or a hand. Some of them wouldn't move at all."

Waiter Henry Bimler had run up the stairs from the kitchen
after trying unsuccessfully to convince the loyal Catherine Swett
to abandon the cash box and save herself. Employee loyalty had
taken a different, more frustrating twist when Henry Bimler
asked for the keys to the locked service door, which he knew

were kept somewhere in the kitchen. Give me the keys, Bimler told an employee he would never identify. "Not until the boss tells me," the employee responded. A stunned Bimler ran back upstairs to join others kicking and pulling at the unresponsive door. Firemen and passersby had found some two-by-fours and finally succeeded in breaking the door, allowing Bimler and a score of others to escape.

As the flames and heat were gradually quelled at the entryways, hose lines were threaded into the club, allowing the firefighters to venture into the interior. District Chief Charles D. Robertson ordered the doors of the New Broadway Lounge removed, and he and his men entered the fire-gutted room that had been brand-new eleven days earlier. Robertson then surveyed the results of the panic and roaring flames that had reigned minutes earlier. The victims "were all tangled up with tables and chairs," he reported later. "They were all in one heap, and we had to separate them to get the bodies out." Robertson made his way toward the L-shaped passageway that connected to the main room. However, as he approached, the fire re-ignited, and the hoses had to be played on it until it was safe to move forward. Robertson entered the now-soggy passageway, which had been completely gutted, and found that it "was full of bodies."

Deputy Chief John McDonough was now making his way through the main entrance on Piedmont Street. There were scores of bodies piled 8 feet high spread around the revolving door, he said. He asked a fireman about conditions in the main dining room and was told, "They were piled up worse than they are here."

At 11:02, McDonough ordered a fifth alarm even though the fire was under control. He needed the extra manpower, the thirty-eight-year veteran said, because his men "were showing signs of being affected by the smoke, gas, and the gruesomeness of things."

Whether he looked to his right, in the direction of the Caricature Bar, or to the left, toward the staircase to the Melody Lounge, McDonough saw that nearly everything in the foyer had been burned, from floor to ceiling. Chairs and settees still lined the foyer walls just as they had before the fire, but now they were desiccated charcoal forms, ready to crumble under the slightest weight.

But as he descended the staircase to the basement, McDonough saw less evidence of fire—only the ceiling and the highest parts of the walls were scorched. There was almost nothing left of the fabric ceiling in the staircase, and this was true of the Melody Lounge's satin ceiling—designer Bodenhorn's "heavens on a starry night." But, except for the ceiling fabric and the ashy remains of the artificial palm tree, the Melody Lounge, more than any other room, looked as it had just before 10:15 P.M. The zebra-striped settees still lined the walls, intact and unburned. The fire had barely touched the octagonal bar and Goodie Goodell's piano. Only a few of the tables and chairs had been scorched.

The fire department's official report would describe the condition of the Melody Lounge as "contrary to usual fire experience." The report observed, "Much of the cloth, rattan, and bamboo contained in the Melody Lounge, and on the sides, and lower walls of the stairway leading therefrom, was, in fact, not burned at all, and the same [was] true of the carpet on the stairway."

In fact, the fire had moved so quickly through—and out of—the Melody Lounge that Daniel Weiss was able to wait it out. Weiss, a medical student who had been hired by his uncle, Barney Welansky, to be the weekend "checker" of the cashiers, emerged with only a sore throat. He had lain on the floor within the bar area for several minutes, covering his mouth and nose with a wet towel. He later estimated that there were practically no flames in the Melody Lounge after three minutes, when he groped through the dark, silent room to make his departure through the door on the back wall leading to the kitchen. Weiss was the last person to leave the Melody Lounge alive.

The difference between what the firemen saw in the Melody Lounge and the more complete devastation they had seen in the foyer and some other areas of the Grove was dictated by the unalterable chemistry of fire.

Chemists employ the four sides of a tetrahedron to describe the elements necessary to create fire—fuel, heat, and oxygen in a combination that creates the fourth element, a chain reaction. When fuel is heated sufficiently in the presence of oxygen—to its "ignition point"—its molecules are broken apart, releasing heat and light, the chain reaction. The additional heat in turn causes further molecular breakup, thus reinforcing the chain reaction, making the fire self-sustaining. The light is seen as flame, which is where the "fire" is actually taking place.

What was burning in the Grove—or interacting with the oxygen—was not the blue satin cloth, the bamboo, or the leatherette, but the flammable gases emitted by those heated fuels. As the oxygen in the fuel itself was used up, the fire sought to draw oxygen from the air around it. That is why air supply was critical in determining the magnitude and the path of the fire in the enclosed space of the Melody Lounge.

The room was, relatively speaking, an oxygen-deficient space—a low-ceilinged, windowless basement. Given the scarcity of oxygen, the gases emitted by the fabric were incompletely burned, but nevertheless extraordinarily hot and toxic. Investigators would conclude that

> a major part of the great volume of burning gas projected to the first floor consisted of carbon monoxide gas. This gas had arisen as a by-product of the fire, burning with [a] deficiency of oxygen in the low-studded room. . . . The fire did not burn itself out in the Melody Lounge primarily because in that confined space it lacked sufficient oxygen for complete combustion, and lacked also adequate means for dissipation of heat produced by the partial combustion which took place.

The nearly universal observations of the survivors tended to confirm this version of events. Most patrons said that the flames along the ceiling of the Melody Lounge were not just blue, but also yellow, white, or orange, an indication of incomplete combustion.

It was superheated smoke—perhaps reaching 1,800 degrees Fahrenheit—and carbon monoxide gas, not flame, that took the heaviest toll in the Melody Lounge. Ruth Strogoff was struck by the way "people were screaming but they seemed to be falling down without even trying to run or push." One of those who dropped where she had been standing next to the bar was Radcliffe student Sydney E. McKenna. Her face was badly burned, but she hadn't been touched by flame. She was taken to Massachusetts General Hospital, where she died three days later. An autopsy would confirm that she had died of pulmonary burns resulting from the inhalation of superheated smoke, which had also burned her face. Others died with no apparent burns from either the flames or the smoke, as Ruth Strogoff had observed.

About forty minutes later, fireman John Collins entered the Melody Lounge and saw the whole picture—lifeless men and women, many apparently unburned, seated at tables or lying where they had been standing. He recalled one victim in particular. "There was a very pretty girl. She was sitting with her eyes open and her hand on a cocktail glass, as if waiting for someone. As I first looked at her, I wondered why she was just sitting there, thinking she was okay. But, of course, she was dead."

The enormous pressure generated by the heat in the Melody Lounge pushed the gases toward the steep public stairway. That stairway, investigators would conclude, then "acted like a chimney, adding the draft of suction to the pressure generated in the room below by heat." The heat pushed the hot gases while the air in the staircase sucked the fire up to the main floor. "Such effect appears to have been very considerable," according to the investigators, "since it drew out the flame entirely, leaving unconsumed [much of] the wood and cloth material."

Once in the foyer, the leatherette wall coverings glued to the walls, "which would be unaffected by ordinary flame such as that from a match, did not withstand this blast of superheated burning gas," according to the investigation. This is where the silent explosion—described by survivors as a "poof"—had occurred.

Joseph Kelly, the observant and articulate Grove patron who had first seen the fire from his seat at the Caricature Bar, noted the "gaseous flame . . . something burning in suspension" in the foyer. "The air itself was full of flames," he reported, "and the walls and ceiling were not then on fire. I believe that some gas generated in the Melody Lounge was burning as it flowed up those stairs."

Years later this phenomenon would be given a name—flashover. Flashover occurs when smoke and combustible gases reach a critical temperature. At this point, the atmosphere explodes and burns independently of the original source at temperatures that may reach 1,800 degrees Fahrenheit.

The fire's progress down the length of the foyer, the investigators said, "appears to have been accelerated by the large ventilating exhaust fan . . . of the Caricature Bar . . . [that] had the effect of increasing the chimney effect of the stairway."

Because the revolving door sealed the fire within the Grove, "the great mass of compressed partially-burned gases spread into the main room and into the Broadway Lounge. . . . In the intense heat which resulted from the progress of the fire, decomposition of practically all combustible material in certain portions of the building resulted."

The damage to the main room was mixed, with some areas completely burned and others seemingly untouched. Nevertheless, because of its immediate proximity to the foyer, the terrace was almost completely devastated, and because the wrought-iron railing penned the guests in, nearly two-thirds of the thirty or so in the Buck Jones party were killed on the spot, and almost all of the survivors required extensive hospitalization. Buck Jones was found alive—but barely so. He was taken to Massachusetts General Hospital where he died of burns and smoke inhalation two days later.

Dead, too, was Bunny Leslie, the club's very atypical cigarette girl. Those who remembered commented that Bunny, who had taken her seat on the terrace where she routinely sat during the floor shows, looked particularly pretty that night in her black evening gown with full skirt and gold-embroidered red jacket. Bunny didn't need to spend each night with the ribbon of her cigarette tray hung around her neck. She came from a well-to-do family, and she bore a remarkable resemblance to her older half-sister, Lillian Roth, a well-known singer and movie star who, most famously, had co-starred with the Marx Brothers in their classic *Animal Crackers*.

Perhaps because of their shared stage-mother, the show business bug had also bitten young Bunny. While waiting to be discovered, she took singing and dancing lessons and reportedly had accumulated more gowns than had any other cigarette girl in town. Sitting on the terrace so close to movie star Buck Jones may have raised her hopes of being discovered. But all hope for both of them died that night on the terrace.

The irony of Buck Jones's death is that if he had followed the original schedule, which would have put him at the USO Buddies Club at 9:30, he would probably not have been in the Grove until well after 10:15. Of course, over the next few days many such ironies were noted. The Boston newspapers would soon be filled with "but for the grace of God" features. There was the doctor who left the Grove early to attend to a birth. There was Sigmund Cohen, who left moments before the fire because "there was something in the air." And Mayor Maurice J. Tobin and Fire Commissioner William A. Reilly would probably have been there too if the hometown favorite hadn't lost the game that afternoon.

Fifteen-year-old Eleanor Chiampa must have been excited to be in the illustrious Cocoanut Grove, sitting on the terrace near a famous movie star. She was among the few people on the terrace who were not part of the Buck Jones contingent. Her big brother, Lieutenant Benjamin Chiampa, and Ben's wife, Giovanna, had brought her to the Grove; the Chiampas were sitting with Adele and Dr. Joseph Dreyfus.

All three women died. Eleanor lingered for several days at Mass General but then became the fire's youngest fatality. An autopsy would reveal a "false membrane" covering her larynx and windpipe, caused by the inhalation of hot smoke. Ben's wife, Giovanna, known to her friends as Jennie, died immediately of severe burns and smoke inhalation. Adele Dreyfus also died immediately. She suffered burns of the face, right shoulder, breasts, arms, buttocks, larynx, trachea, and bronchi.

As District Chief Robertson had observed, the passageway to the New Broadway Lounge was completely incinerated, the outlines of this corridor barely discernible. Inside the new lounge itself, "I found one body completely devoid of flesh and wedged into a telephone booth," Robertson reported. However, the checkroom, on a side wall and out of the line of the fire, was intact.

While the firemen inside the Grove buildings went about their tasks with a grim calm, there was wild confusion outside. The square block around the Grove and adjoining streets were quickly choked with emergency vehicles, hoses, ladders, and tools. The fire department would bring in twenty-five engine companies, a rescue company, five ladder companies, and a water tower.

Parked vehicles were pushed aside or crushed by the fire trucks moving into position. Beams from giant floodlights cut through the thick smoke and reflected against the icy pools of water from the fire hoses on this 28-degree night. Makeshift dressing stations and morgues were set up in area garages, in hotel lobbies, and in private homes. Police vehicles, ambulances, taxicabs, and newspaper delivery trucks burrowed into the area to carry victims to hospitals or to the Northern and Southern Mortuaries.

A huge crowd was building on the streets. Drawn by the glow of the fire and the beams of the floodlights, curiosity seekers, frantic friends, relatives, and volunteers quickly intermingled with the police, firemen, and stunned survivors.

Overburdened police organized groups of servicemen to lock arms and push the onlookers back, and the frontline of rescuers became an ad-hoc mix of city personnel, military men and women, and civilians. As the heat and smoke cleared, these random groups of rescuers gathered around smashed doors and windows, peeling victims off sidewalks or passing them hand to hand directly from the Grove to be packed into any available vehicle. Bodies were still being removed from the Grove at 1:35 A.M. when martial law was declared in the area.

At the same time, many of the survivors who could walk were pushing through the assembling crowd in search of their companions, as were Mildred Jeffers and Louis Hern after they were separated from their spouses. Other survivors were hysterical. Nina Underwood, a twenty-year-old Red Cross volunteer, reported, "I had to knock down a girl and a man with jiu jitsu because they were out of control." The girl was "pretty high with liquor," Nina said.

Nina Underwood also described how "the service men constantly had to forcibly restrain people from plunging back into the building." Clifford Johnson was one who succeeded in plunging back. The young Coast Guardsman from rural Missouri had been in the New Broadway Lounge with Estelle Balkan. Like many others, he had been overpowered by the scrambling crowd and pushed unscathed through the exit onto Broadway. But, also like many others, his companion's hand had been wrenched from his grasp. Estelle, to whom he had been introduced by a mutual friend only that afternoon, was trapped inside.

Johnson turned around, climbed over the accumulating bodies in the vestibule, and then pushed his way through the inward-closing door to search for her. He tried this four times but could not find Estelle. After his fourth attempt, he emerged a ball of flame and fell to the sidewalk. He had deep dermal burns over more than half of his body. Rescuers later found Estelle Balkan, alive but badly injured. Johnson was still alive, but just barely. He was rushed to Boston City Hospital.

He would become a medical miracle.

Francis D. Moore and his friend Charles Burbank, young surgical residents at Massachusetts General Hospital, were in charge of the emergency room this Saturday night. It had been a quiet shift, and at about 10:30 they were in an upstairs lounge listening to a football game on the radio. They were only slightly distracted by the commonplace sound of a single ambulance siren. However, the second, third, and fourth sirens were impossible to ignore, and they hurried down the stairs toward the ER.

In the time it had taken the doctors to rouse themselves, bodies had already been lined up in neat rows in the hallway. More than fifty years later, Dr. Moore could still recall being greeted by "that smell of burnt clothes and hair."

Within the next hour, 114 victims would be brought to Mass General. Moore and Burbank's first job was to separate the living from the dead—and the viable from the dying. Of those 114, seventy-five were either already dead or would die within minutes or hours.

Contrary to popular imagery, the body of the common burn fatality is not always char-black, although that can happen if the flesh actually ignites as a result of body fat melting into clothing and producing a "wick" effect. Instead, in most cases the body is, in the jaded parlance of pathologists, "parboiled" or "stewed in its own juices"—bloated, intensely red, and blistered. In more severe cases, the skin becomes yellow-brown and leathery. The contracted skin will split, exposing desiccated muscle and tissue. The enormous heat of a fire may cause the skull to flake off, or the soft tissues and bone to be burned, causing hands, feet, arms, or legs to separate from the body. Body hair, being the most easily flammable, if not burned away, is melted into clumps.

The heat of the fire causes the muscles to shorten, with the result that the victim's arms may be bent at the elbows, with wrists turned inward, and knees bent, giving the body the boxer's stance, or "pugilist's attitude." The first victim he saw looked just this way to Deputy Chief John McDonough as he stood outside the remnants of the revolving door. "The fire was coming out the main door. . . . I saw a body lying there. I thought it was a statue for a minute," said McDonough. McDonough ordered a hose played on the doorway, crawled under the flames, and pulled out the stiffened body. He never learned whether the rigid form was a man or woman.

From observing the telltale signs, Moore and Burbank quickly concluded that respiratory damage had taken an even larger toll than had dermal burns. The skin and lips of some of the victims had turned deep blue. They had suffocated in the purest sense, drowned by smoke. The fire had consumed most of the available oxygen and left little to breath.

Others were a cherry pink color, an almost healthy glow about them. They had died from carbon monoxide poisoning. Fire in an enclosed space, where the oxygen is being consumed, forms carbon monoxide, a gas that has an affinity for blood hemoglobin hundreds of times greater than oxygen. As a result, the body's tissues starve for lack of oxygen and die—a chemical asphyxiation.

Still other victims were frothy about the mouth. They had died from pulmonary edema, a pneumonia-like drowning caused by the lungs filling up with bubbly bloody fluids in response to the inhalation of the irritant gases emitted by the wood, fabric, and leatherette. Many of these victims had burns and soot stains on their lips and in their nostrils and mouth. This was a sure sign of severe burns to, and blockage of, the air passageway, like a powerful hand pinching their throats shut. Some of these victims also had burns about the face and neck, causing what Dr. Moore would recall as "grotesque swelling" that further pressed against their windpipes.

Of course, victims do not fall neatly into discreet categories, and many had died from a deadly combination of respiratory and dermal complications. Some had fallen victim to the smoke and heat and then were burned. Although he was not dead on arrival—he would live for forty hours—Buck Jones was probably a typical victim in many ways. His autopsy report documented that he had first-, second-, and third-degree burns covering his entire face and upper neck, with the third-degree

burns localized around his mouth, nose, chin, and ears. His entire face was swollen. Burns also covered the backs of his hands,
the result of his efforts to protect his face. His throat had been
all but sealed shut, with the obstruction so great that, even after
performing a tracheotomy, doctors were unable to establish an
airway to his lungs. Nevertheless, even if they had been able to
open his airway, his body was unable to absorb oxygen. His lung
tissues were "drowned by massive pulmonary edema," his air
sacs filled with frothy fluid—"only at the periphery of the lungs
were there narrow aerated zones."

Many of the patients were in severe pain. Pain control of
burn patients is not only humane, it is part of burn therapy,
helping to reduce the elevated state of anxiety and thereby aid-
ing in controlling the complex of the body's reactions to burn
trauma. But an overdose of morphine can cause respiratory arrest. During the hectic initial stages, nurses used their lipsticks
to mark an "M" on the foreheads of patients who had been administered morphine. "But this was not always clear," recalled
Dr. Moore, "and sometimes a second or even third dose of
morphine was given. One or two may have died of this overdose. We never knew."

At Massachusetts General Hospital 39 of the 114 victims
lived through the night; 29 had lung injuries, and 10 were severely burned. The scene was even drearier at Boston City Hospital, the city's public hospital: 300 victims were brought there,
168 dead on arrival. Of the 132 still alive, 36 died within hours.
It was later estimated that during the first hour or so after the
fire, victims were arriving at Boston City Hospital at the rate of
one every eleven seconds. By 11:30, officials at Boston City
passed the word that they could not accept any more victims.

Some victims were taken to other civilian and military hospitals in the Boston area, but Boston City and Mass General bore the brunt of the emergency. Studies of the London Blitz and other civilian disasters suggested that living casualties would outnumber the dead by three to one. However, the ratio was nearly reversed on that night—as the death toll pushed toward 500, with fewer than 200 surviving victims. The hard truth was that during the early hours, precious time was lost in examining those who were already dead. Doctors were soon dispatched to the Grove with the sole task of separating the living from the dead.

All of this was taking place while many uninjured—or apparently uninjured—people were also pouring through the doors of the two hospitals in search of their loved ones and companions. Some were out of control. Dr. Moore recalled one naval officer who was among those looking for his family at Mass General, evidently unaware of his own pulmonary injuries. He ran up and down the hallways looking for them until he fell to the floor, spitting up the froth that had been filling his lungs to capacity, and died.

CHAPTER 7

It's Not My Job

We will dig down to the last grain of sand and no one will be spared.

Massachusetts Attorney General
Robert T. Bushnell

Reilly, in response to several inquiries from newspapermen, asserted he wanted to give emphatic denial to any report that he expected Mayor Tobin to give evidence to the inquest.

Boston Herald, *December 10, 1942*

IT HAD BEGUN WITH the Eighteenth Amendment. According to Jack Beatty's definitive biography of James Michael Curley,* during the Prohibition years of 1920 to 1933, the small city of Boston had at least four thousand speakeasies—one illegal establishment for about every 185 persons—four of them on the same street as the central police station. Beatty quotes the

---

*Jack Beatty, *The Rascal King* (New York: DaCapo, 2000).

mayor of Boston, *England*, after returning from a good-will visit in 1930, saying of Boston, *Massachusetts*, "You can swim in liquor. . . . You can drown yourself in it." Beatty described how the rascally Curley had demonstrated his disdain for the Noble Experiment by attaching a corkscrew and bottle opener to the keys to the city he handed out to visiting dignitaries.

Many politicians had made their fortunes by looking the other way during the "old days" that had ended barely nine years earlier. The bond between public officials and nightclub operators, a bond somewhere between bribery and extortion, did not die with repeal, and the memory of those associations would be quickly recalled after the fire.

Mayor Maurice J. Tobin and Fire Commissioner William Arthur Reilly must have spent the early hours of Sunday morning contemplating just such uncomfortable recollections. Their concerns were well founded. Reilly later acknowledged his and the mayor's discomfort in his department's annual report for 1942. "Soon afterwards," the commissioner wrote, "the Fire Department bore the brunt of the blame, followed by others, department by department, and official by official. . . . Surging onward and upward the wave of censure inundated even . . . the Mayor."

Within days after the fire, Albert West, a Boston attorney and reformer, called on "all citizens who are unhampered by political activity" to "rise as one and insist that the existing laws be enforced with rigid impartiality." The fire was "a horrible indictment of the city's political mismanagement," he said. West added that the Welansky family members were "intimate friends" of the mayor. In addition, under the heading of the pot calling the kettle black, former lieutenant governor

Francis E. Kelley, a political foe of Tobin and Reilly, announced that he would propose a bill to the state legislature requiring that the Boston fire commissioner be a civil service employee taken from the ranks of the department. The catastrophe could have been prevented by "a competent fire commissioner," said Kelley.

Robert S. Moulton, technical secretary of the National Fire Protection Association, blasted Boston's fire laws and the politicians charged with their enforcement. The laws were, he said, "in a chaotic condition" and subject to "incompetent enforcement, political influence, and careless management."

The national and local press joined in pointing the finger of blame at city officials, who were running for cover behind what they described as vague laws and regulations. *The Christian Science Monitor* complained, "The process of whitewashing is sickening. . . . Dine-dance-drink places have too often been closely connected with politicians. . . . For a generation Boston has been satisfied with government on the nightclub and racetrack level." The *New York Times* said the blame "falls on the proprietors of the establishment *and* on the city officials of Boston." The *Boston Herald* editorialized, "There are laws that could and should have been enforced" that "would have prevented this unspeakable, indefensible calamity." The essayist Bernard De Voto, writing in *Harper's Magazine*, said that "one reason why law and regulations can be disregarded with impunity is that some of those charged with the duty of enforcing them make a living from not enforcing them."

Then there was the nagging Republican Massachusetts attorney general, Robert T. Bushnell. The attorney general announced that his office and the Suffolk County district attorney would conduct a joint investigation and that, without doubt, there would be indictments. He too pointed the finger at Boston's officialdom. "It is well to bear in mind," Bushnell's statement read, "that whenever such tragedies occur there is a tendency to look for the cause in defects of statutory law. This has occurred not infrequently when it has been quite obvious that diligent enforcement of the law as it then existed could have prevented the tragedy then under discussion."

Bushnell served his ominous notice that the investigation would "dig down to the last grain of sand and no one will be spared . . . whether he be an official or private citizen."

On December 1, three days after the fire, Bushnell formally began his inquiry, and the city's newspapers immediately began speculating about unnamed politicians. "Public Officials Face Indictment," announced a *Boston Herald* headline, while a *Boston Globe* front-page story asked, "Were any profits of the club paid to any political figures?"

The four morning papers submitted a joint list of questions to the attorney general that suggested who they thought these un-named officials might be. The papers asked pointedly whether these officials would be called: Mayor Tobin, Fire Commissioner Reilly, Police Commissioner Timilty, building department Commissioner Mooney, and chair of the Boston licensing board, Mary Driscoll. Another question put by the pool of reporters suggested a financial tie between the Welanskys and the mayor: "Have you had State House or any other public records examined to determine what political contributions were made by the management of the Cocoanut Grove . . . to Boston political campaigns?" The attorney general declined to respond to the questions, citing the imminent grand jury proceeding, but

Reilly must have felt the steamy breath of Robert Tyng Bushnell on his neck.

The press discovered that in 1938 the state legislature had enacted a revision to Boston's 1907 building code. This somewhat more stringent enabling legislation required formal adoption by the city. Mayor Tobin claimed it had been under study for the past four years. However, the word was out that Tobin had pigeonholed the bill because he had not wanted to incur the wrath of the propertied interests who had put him into office.

William Arthur Reilly's son, a young boy at the time, recalls that his father barely made it home the morning after the fire. After having spent the night commiserating with his boss, Mayor Tobin, at the fire, the two men then visited the Northern and Southern Mortuaries to view the dead lying on tile floors and on slabs. He and Tobin did their best to console the distraught relatives who had gone from hospital to hospital before making the final dreaded trip to the mortuaries. That morning, Reilly returned home briefly for a change of clothes and then headed back to the fire department headquarters at 60 Bristol Street.

The morning papers had hit the stands and screamed out the horror stories of the fire, with the total deaths variously estimated in the 400s. The final death toll would be at least 490.*

---

*To this day, the number of dead is variously given as 490, 491, or 492. The Boston fire department's report, dated nearly a full year after the fire, and presumably complete, indicates "490 deaths and 166 injuries." However, some newspaper stories had listed William "Bubbles" Shea, the corpulent New Broadway Lounge bartender who died in February, as the 491st death. Similarly, the final fatality, Phyllis Atkins, who died in May, is sometimes described as the 492nd victim. Most contemporary accounts use the figure of 492, even though Shea and Atkins are included among the 490 dead in the fire department's report.

About twelve hours after the fire, the fire commissioner re-luctantly took his place on center stage at fire department head-quarters. Late Sunday morning, he convened the first of what would become an extraordinary series of public hearings, com-piling well over a thousand pages of testimony.

Initially, Reilly attempted to resolve his various dilemmas by declaring the hearings closed—claiming that they were "a sort of an inquest," like a grand jury proceeding. The Boston newspapers complained, and Mayor Tobin was forced to order his fire com-missioner to conduct the hearings in public sessions. Reilly saved face by stating at the opening of the hearings that, in view of the large loss of life, "we have made an exception to ordinary rule and allowed representatives of the press to the hearing." The fifteen reporters at the first hearing outnumbered the witnesses.

The first witnesses to give testimony on Sunday were the fire department brass who had supervised the response. Laying the basis for what was to become an official defense, Reilly asked each of the chiefs and deputy chiefs the same question: Was there evidence of panic? Of course, each answered in the affir-mative. Aside from Chief McDonough noting that the emer-gency door at the top of the Melody Lounge staircase was locked, there was no discussion of exits, overcrowding, or flam-mable materials.

Despite Reilly's obvious ambivalence, he would soon be un-able to control the flow of embarrassing disclosures. Under the daily scrutiny of the local and national press, the hearings were completely unscripted, with no pre-screening or off-the-record testimony. As a result, one day's revelations would raise new pointed questions that the commissioner would be forced to pursue the next day.

On Monday, November 30, the first of what were to prove several star witnesses testified. Sixteen-year-old bar boy Stanley F. Tomaszewski, the hapless young man who had been instructed by barman John Bradley to turn on the light in the palm tree, took the stand. His face frozen in fright and confusion as he was sworn in, Stanley must have begun at that moment to sense the specter that would haunt him for the rest of his life. After all, hadn't he killed all those people? Some people thought so. On Sunday, Police Commissioner Joseph F. Timilty had told the press that Stanley had started the blaze accidentally. And immediately before Stanley's testimony, fire department Chief Samuel J. Pope testified that, based on information he had received from the police, he agreed. Nearly all of the Monday morning city newspapers printed stories like the *Herald*'s, which announced, "Bus Boy Fixing Light with Match Set Fire."

But Stanley was an unlikely villain. One of his teachers had described him as "one of the swellest kids." The handsome, strapping Stanley was an honor student at the Roxbury Memorial High School for Boys, his classroom's treasurer for buying war bonds, a first-string tackle on the football team, and an officer in his school's junior cadet program. He had worked nine-hour-plus shifts from 4 P.M. until after 1 A.M. on Friday and Saturday nights for $2.47 per night plus tips. Most of what he made went to help his sick mother and his father, a janitor. Any money left over after helping his family, Stanley had used to purchase war stamps and bonds. On Sunday, he had voluntarily walked into a police station to report on his role in the fire.

Reilly demonstrated an almost parental concern for the boy. Before calling him to testify, Reilly did what he could to make

Stanley as comfortable as possible under the circumstances. "He, of his own volition, went to Police Station 4 and volunteered information concerning this fire," Reilly announced. And he admonished the press, "He is 16 years old . . . so if you are going to take any pictures, take them and get them over with, so we won't disturb his testimony." Then he turned to the boy and told him, "You can just relax, because there is nobody here who is going to cause you any bother or any trouble at all."

Seeming "older than his years," according to the *Herald*, Stanley explained how he had mounted the stool to find the loosened bulb near the top of the palm tree, how he had struck a match to find it—the only bulb in the tree and in that now-darkened corner. "I shook it like, to put it out, and then I stepped on it. I was told not to lay any matches lighted on the floor; to make sure they are out," he said. Then, almost immediately, the tree and satin ceiling were ablaze, said Stanley. "It was worse than any gasoline fire that I've ever seen," he reported.

Reilly then asked, "Do you think the match could have caused the tree to catch fire?" "I don't know," he answered. Reilly gently let this pardonable evasion pass unquestioned. But later he put the same question more obliquely: "Do you think the fire started at that palm tree where the light was?" "I think so," he replied.

After explaining that he had run up the service stairs with several patrons whom he had led out of the Melody Lounge and out through an exit that he didn't identify, Stanley told how he had spent the rest of the night and the next morning searching for his pal and classmate, Joe Tranfaglia.

Joe was also sixteen years old and had been the person who had got him the job at the Grove. He went to Joe's house first and was told by Joe's parents that he hadn't come home. On Sunday, he searched everywhere—or nearly everywhere. "I went to City Hospital, Massachusetts General Hospital, and then I went to Police Headquarters," he said, but he couldn't find his friend. Like hundreds of others, Stanley may have been reluctant to go to the Southern Mortuary, just across from Boston City Hospital, perhaps afraid of what he might find. If he had gone there, he would have found the body of his friend Joe.

Reilly heaped praise on Stanley, telling the shaken youth that he had "done an honorable thing" by coming forward to testify. The *Boston Herald* editorialized the next day that Stanley should be "forgiven and forgotten. He must not, of course, be made a scapegoat. He is a clean, intelligent lad, and he made an excellent impression in his frank testimony yesterday." In the ensuing days, letters poured into the newspapers defending Stanley. "The blame should not be on the shoulders of this 16-year-old boy," read one typical letter to the *Boston Globe*, "but rather on the heads of the all the corrupt officials whose hands were greased with money." Another citizen wrote, "Boston has long had . . . a corrupt system of 'string pulling.' . . . The building and fire inspectors have many terrible questions to answer."

Despite such overwhelming sympathy for the young man—who, at age sixteen, was illegally employed at a place where alcohol was served—Stanley's life was threatened, and he would be kept at the Kenmore Hotel under protective police guard for the next several months.

Earlier in the day, Lieutenant Frank J. Linney, a fire department inspector, had given testimony, and this had been the first of Reilly's awkward moments. Linney had visited the Grove on November 20, just eight days before the fire, and given new meaning to the phrase "routine inspection." The typed one-page report, on the "Fire Prevention Division" letterhead, signed with the neat signature of "Frank J. Linney, Lieutenant," would be reprinted in the next edition of virtually every Boston daily paper. This record of the fire department "inspection" quickly became the city's visual metaphor for political corruption. Linney's report stated that there was "no inflammable decoration" and a "sufficient number of exits."

As to the lack of flammable decoration, Linney testified that he had only tested the trees in the main dining room, not the ceiling fabric and not any part of the Melody Lounge. He had taken off some of the fake bark from the columns and touched a match to it. "These were treated to my satisfaction," he said. This account was greeted with skepticism in light of the fact that another of those trees had failed the same "test" under Stanley Tomaszewski's match only eight days later.

Linney also offered a strange assessment on the adequacy of the exits. When asked about his "sufficient exits" notation, he explained that, for instance, a second-floor window in the dressing room through which one might climb up to the roof (without the benefit of a fire escape) was a sufficient exit. The waiter Charles Mikalonis, "hypnotized" by panic, had climbed through this window before he dangled by his fingertips off the roof's edge and then fell to the ground.

Reilly asked his subordinate, "And do you still feel in the light of what happened that the condition of the premises was good on November 20 when you inspected the premises?" "Positively," he replied.

"And that there was nothing that would lead you to believe that a fire, a small fire breaking out in the premises, would spread as rapidly as apparently this fire did?" Reilly pushed.

"If there was, I would have seen that he had a notice to abate condition," Linney responded.

Meanwhile, Boston's city agencies were suddenly flexing new-found muscle. The Boston licensing board ordered 1,161 night-clubs, restaurants, and hotels to suspend all dancing and entertainment until the Boston building department had inspected them. (By banning entertainment, the board hoped to keep the crowds down until the inspections were completed.) The next day the board went further and ordered fifty-one nightclubs closed entirely, pending inspections. In addition, Mayor Tobin ordered the removal of all revolving doors from Boston City Hall.

For his part, Reilly discovered that, after all, he did have the authority to ban flammable decorations in public places, and he issued a ban on flammable materials for all the city's "stores, halls, and places of public assembly," effective through the Christmas–New Year season. State regulations had been issued eight months earlier that clearly charged the fire department with the responsibility for seeing that public places had unobstructed exits and no flammable decorations. The question hung in the air: Why hadn't Reilly enforced the law before the fire?

The subject of flammable materials in the Grove was central to the testimony of designer Reuben O. Bodenhorn. As flamboyant as his name, Bodenhorn had designed nearly every important nightclub in Boston by 1942. In addition to the Grove, he had worked his magic at the Mayfair, Versailles, Music Box, Club Touraine, Brunswick, Roseland Ballroom,

Lafayette, Bostonian, and Latin Quarter (both in New York and Boston). "Well, it is sort of disgusting . . . ," Bodenhorn said with disingenuous modesty after reciting the list of his design commissions.

Bodenhorn, who claimed he kept no records, invoices, or contracts, testified that he had always ordered flame-retardant fabric for the Grove, and as far as he knew, that's what was installed. "Were any tests made of this flameproofed material?"

"That I don't know," Bodenhorn answered.

"When you specified flameproof material, you presumed it was, and didn't test it?"

"Yes."

His subcontractors would unintentionally undermine Bodenhorn's assertion. Materials supplier and installer Joseph Dobesch testified confidently that Bodenhorn had indeed been correct; all of the satin materials in the Grove's Melody Lounge, the staircase, and the main dining room had been flameproofed. When asked how he knew this, Dobesch responded that the manufacturers' invoices clearly indicated that the material had been properly treated. However, when he produced the invoices, there was no indication of the treatment whatsoever. Hyman Horowitz, whose firm had supplied the Grove with much of its leatherette and bamboo, further cast Bodenhorn's credibility into question. Horowitz explained that any materials shipped by his company that were flameproof were so marked and that none shipped to the Grove were so labeled. "Therefore, none of them was flameproof," said Horowitz.

Finally, chemist Andrew Landini refuted Bodenhorn's claims scientifically. His firm tested samples of all of the various materials actually taken from the Grove. The report stated that the fake bark around the structural columns in the main dining room—the material that Lieutenant Frank Linney had claimed he tested with a match—"burned like a dry Christmas tree." Landini also found that the satin used on the ceilings and the stage curtains "burst into flame almost instantly and was entirely consumed." The red leatherette from the Caricature Bar "ignited readily and was consumed quickly," emitting "very irritating acrid fumes . . . which we believe to be oxides of nitrogen."

Bodenhorn had also claimed that the allegedly flame-retardant satin material on the ceiling had been periodically re-treated after its installation with a flame-retardant chemical. Landini took fabric samples from the Melody Lounge identical to the ones that he had observed "instantly" bursting into flame. After these samples were treated with the chemical that allegedly had been used in the club, they did not burn, suggesting strongly that the materials in the Grove had never been treated or re-treated.

Specific evidence and testimony now demonstrated what everyone had known instinctively: No materials in the club had been flame retardant, notwithstanding Linney and Bodenhorn's claims to the contrary. Reilly had prefaced his questioning of Linney and Bodenhorn by warning them, "Anything you say in this instance may be used against you later." His words would prove prophetic.

James H. Mooney, the building commissioner, whose department had allowed the New Broadway Lounge to open without fusible doors and a new fire exit and without a final inspection, testified that there was a loophole in the law that prevented him from mandating fire exits at the Grove. He asserted that his authority extended to places of "public assembly," such as theaters. What was the difference? The Grove was a restaurant, he said, and because it did not charge for admission, it was not a place of public assembly. His chief responsibility, said Mooney, was to see that walls and roofs were properly constructed. "And that's about all." He offered the opinion that, in any event, there were plenty of exits in the Grove for nearly 1,400 people, though he failed to note that most of the exits were locked, blocked, or obscured.

Mooney also reiterated the theme struck by Reilly on the first day of the hearings, suggesting that the dead were responsible for their own misfortune because they had panicked. He then went on to offer one of the most bizarre opinions of the hearing: "I don't believe a panicked crowd would get out even if there were no exterior walls. They would get entangled among themselves and not get out anyway." He also suggested that a single exit could serve as an exit for two spaces. The door from the Melody Lounge to the kitchen behind it could be counted as an exit for both the Melody Lounge and the kitchen, he said. (Fire protection experts retorted that this was an absurd contention because a fire exit, by definition, must get people *out* of a burning building, not to another part of it.)

After his appearance, "Mooney was asked flatly [by a *Boston Herald* reporter] if Mayor Tobin or any other official had ever asked him to 'go easy' in the enforcement of building laws. He replied with considerable vigor: 'No. I refuse to discuss it.'"

The testimony demonstrated that the Grove held, from floor to ceiling, flammable decorations and that its exits were inadequate. But what about the overcrowding? There would be a stark discrepancy between the customers' perception and the testimony of employees. One after another, the patrons described how the place was "jammed," "you couldn't move," "the tables were jammed together," "the crowd made me nervous," "people were nearly on top of each other." By contrast, the employees, who probably were used to the crowds, tended to describe the situation as "not unusual," "a typical Saturday night crowd." Perhaps both were correct. On certain evenings, the place was overcrowded, and this was not unusual. The Grove's 1942 license application stated that there were 460 seats in the club—about thirty fewer than the number of people who died in the fire.

Since 1906 Louis Epple had been the secretary of the Boston licensing board, the agency responsible for issuing liquor licenses and supervising its licensees. The *Boston Globe* would observe that Epple provided the "sole general laugh of the day's hearings" when he stated that the board considered the Cocoanut Grove to be not a nightclub but a restaurant "pure and simple." Epple's testimony was a litany of nine years of nonfeasance: They issued the Grove's liquor license in 1933 without a hearing, due to the pressure of the board's workload during the year of repeal of Prohibition. They had routinely renewed the license annually since then, also without hearings and irrespective of the extensive renovations.

Epple was asked about the description of total occupancy in the license applications: "Suppose you had twice as many people as you should have—what would you do about it?"

Epple replied: "I want to call your attention to all of these applications . . . they are made out under pains of penalty of perjury. I think you noticed that, didn't you? Every application."

At this point in the hearings, every agency had avoided direct responsibility. The building commissioner had said that he had no authority over exits at restaurants and suggested that they might be the responsibility of the fire department. The licensing board thought that the responsibility for exits and overcrowding lay with either the fire department or the building department, but certainly not with its agency.

How could such general nonfeasance have occurred? Harry Weene, a neon lighting specialist, provided the bombshell testimony that hinted how things were done by the well connected. Weene testified that in October he had been called by Barney Welansky to review the lighting plans for the New Broadway Lounge. Bodenhorn had mandated that the corners and ceiling of the modernistic new room be lined by neon piping. Weene went to the New Broadway Lounge and met with Barney and Raymond Baer, whom Barney described as the house "electrician." (Baer was actually a shipfitter in the Boston Navy Yard, part of Barney's stable of occasional workmen.) Weene examined the plans and told Barney and Baer that work this complex required a city permit and supervision by a licensed electrician, which Baer was not.

Weene testified, "Mr. Welansky said that it would not be necessary because 'Mayor Tobin and I fit.'" Weene would later explain that Barney had added, "They owe me plenty." Reilly must have squirmed in his seat, but he moved on to other witnesses and subjects. *The Christian Science Monitor* noted, "The witness did not elaborate on his answer, nor was he asked to do so by Commissioner Reilly."

What Reilly did in response to Weene's statement was to turn the questioning over to Bernard Whelan, the fire department's chief wiring inspector. Whelan's hostile questions aimed at undermining Weene's credibility by demonstrating that he had supervised substandard installations at the Grove and at other locations. Whelan concluded the most hostile questioning of the hearings with the statement, "Well, no wonder you haven't got an electrician's license."

When reporters confronted the mayor with Weene's testimony, Tobin was ready with his denial: "Whether or not Mr. Welansky made this statement, I do not know, but certainly if he did, he had no right to make it, any more than any other man in business has a right to make any other similar statement with regard to me. In my capacity as Mayor of Boston, I am acquainted with hundreds of men operating hundreds of different forms of businesses, and if any one of these men should trade upon my name, or use my name unfairly, it is something beyond my control." Tobin's thorough denial even extended to his *unconscious* mistakes: "I want the people of Boston to know that since I have held the office of Mayor, I have never, wittingly or unwittingly, permitted any winking at the law or any violation of the law."

Every newspaper trumpeted Weene's accusation that Welansky had claimed that his connections had made compliance with the law "not necessary." While the papers noted Tobin's categorical denial, Weene's testimony fueled speculation that the mayor might be indicted.

Reilly must have wondered and worried, *if Tobin goes, what about me?*

Reilly would issue his report almost a year later. In his introduction, he said his public hearings had run from the day after the fire until January 20, 1943, which was inaccurate. In fact, right after Weene's testimony on December 8, Reilly declared that the public hearings would be suspended so that they would not interfere with or compromise the attorney general's investigation. Thereafter, testimony was taken privately.

The outburst by Army Air Corps Private Francis Judeikis, husband of one of the victims, was typical of the public's opinion that the foxes were investigating the misfortune at the henhouse. He complained that "politicians with buttered palms" were conducting the investigation.

CHAPTER 8

Present at the Creation

The next thing I know, John Walsh was slapping me in
the kisser.

Grove emcee Mickey Alpert

THE GROVE'S NOMINAL bandleader, Mickey Alpert, had
been scheduled to testify before Reilly on Monday but had
begged off until Thursday, sending word that he was too ill
from the effects of the fire to leave home. The usually meticulously groomed Alpert, whom most Grove patrons had seen
only in a dinner jacket, appeared before Reilly disheveled and
exhausted. He wore a grimy bandage on his arm, and his hair
was tousled and appeared grayer than usual. He sat slumped,
pulling himself to the witness table with his elbows. His friends
claimed that Mickey had lost twenty pounds in the four days
since the fire.

Mickey recited how he had been seated with Billy Payne, taking advantage of the tardiness of the chorus, when he first saw
the fire thundering into the dining room through the foyer and
from the Caricature Bar. He explained that he had taken the
route down the steps in front of the terrace, then through the

kitchen to the staircase back up to the service door. This door was locked, said Mickey, and he moved into an adjoining room where he found a window to the street. He didn't recall what happened then, he said, or whether he climbed or was pulled through the window. "The next thing I know, John Walsh [the director of public safety, who had been a patron] was slapping me in the kisser," he said.

In the days since the fire, Alpert's public image had suffered mightily. First, there was the unfortunate newspaper photograph of Mickey standing outside the Grove bundled in a woman's white fur coat and looking terrified. Then there were the reporters' snide references to the "once debonair" Mickey seeming haggard and distracted the day before, when he had testified before the separate Bushnell probe. He had shown up that day leaning on the arm of his brother, George Alpert, a former assistant district attorney. The *Boston Herald* reported that Mickey's "hysterical recital of Saturday night's tragedy could be heard outside of the hearing room."

Had Mickey failed his own test of manly obligation to his patrons? Did John Walsh slap him in the kisser because he was unconscious or because he was hysterical? And what had he done to make it out safely, who had he pushed aside, who had he stepped on, whose hair did he pull as he "swam" past the others? On the other hand, perhaps Mickey was distressed by the fear that when the tangled web of the ownership of the Grove was unraveled, he would be shown to bear some responsibility for this awful night.

Whatever his state of mind, Mickey gave carefully tailored responses to Reilly's questions, perhaps upon the advice of his brother George. He mentioned in passing, "I've been there

MAIN FLOORPLAN

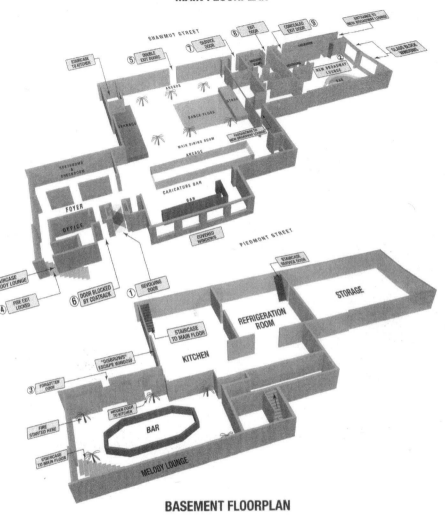

BASEMENT FLOORPLAN

1. Revolving door - Main Entrance
2. Interior door to/from New Broadway Lounge
3. "Forgotten" door behind Melody Lounge
4. Locked emergency door at top of Melody Lounge staircase
5. Double doors (one bolted) behind Venetian doors and blocked by tables
6. Door next to revolving door, locked, blocked by coat rack
7. Service door, locked
8. Additional exit, locked
9. Planned "Emergency Exit" from New Broadway Lounge, locked, hidden behind checkroom

Jack Berman, aka Jack Bennett, aka John Roth, the Julian Petroleum swindler who was the original owner of the Grove.

Charles "King" Solomon, Grove owner during its speakeasy days, from 1930 until his murder in January 1933.

bert F. Callahan and Barney Welansky (Courtesy William Noonan, Boston Fire
artment)

Jimmy Welansky
(Courtesy William Noonan,
Boston Fire Department)

Mayor Maurice J. Tobin (standing) and Fire Commissioner William Arthur Reilly (Court William Noonan, Boston Fire Department)

Attorney General
Robert Tyng Bushnell

rightened sixteen-year-old Stanley Tomaszewski at the Reilly hearing. (Courtesy William
onan, Boston Fire Department)

e Grove's flamboyant designer, Reuben O. Bodenhorn. (Courtesy William Noonan,
ston Fire Department)

A young Angelo Lippi, the Grove maître d', poses in the main dining room during better days. (Courtesy William Noonan, Boston Fire Department)

Mickey Alpert, Grove orchestra leader and second owner of the Grove, posing with cast members of "This Is the Army" early in the evening of the fire. (Courtesy William Noonan, Boston Fire Department)

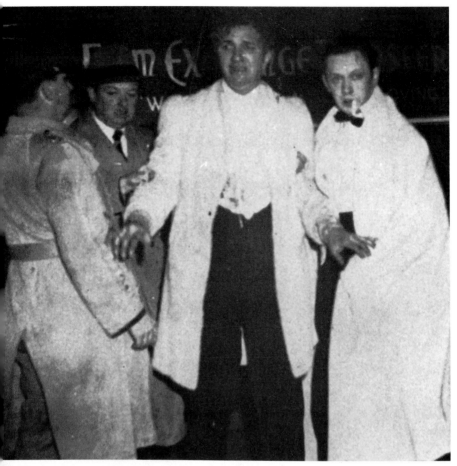

his picture of a terrified Mickey Alpert (center) outside the Grove during the fire in a
oman's fur coat was widely published by the Boston newspapers. Mickey, perhaps
ncerned that his former ownership of the Grove might result in legal responsibility for the
e, would soon leave Boston forever. (Courtesy William Noonan, Boston Fire Department)

Cocoanut Grove
menu cover

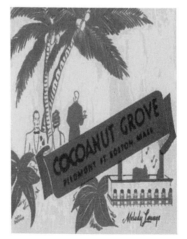

Firemen, policemen, servicemen, and civilians helping to remove victims to Shawmut Street through the broken plate-glass windows, which were covered on the inside by wood paneling. (Courtesy William Noonan, Boston Fire Department)

he sealed, curtained windows in the Caricature Bar area were broken in order to get the tims to Piedmont Street. Before the firemen arrived, Coastguardsman Raymond Carter s the only person who managed to break through one of these windows to safety. ourtesy William Noonan, Boston Fire Department)

PPOSITE PAGE
ictims on Piedmont Street. This picture captures e pandemonium on the streets adjoining the Grove.
ourtesy William Noonan, Boston Fire Department)

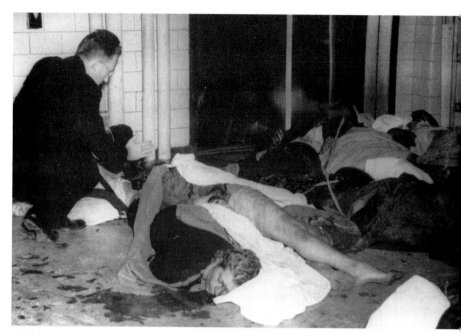

Priest administering last rites at Boston City Hospital. (Courtesy William Noonan, Boston Fire Department)

The grisly job of identifying victims at the Northern Mortuary. (Courtesy William Noonan, Boston Fire Department)

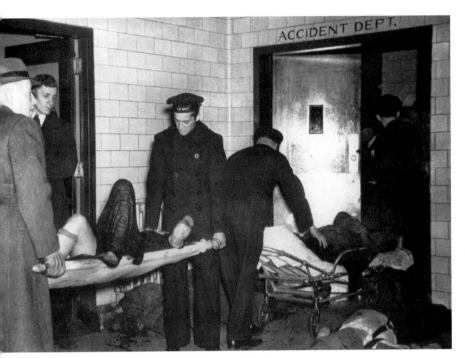

The scene at the Boston City Hospital emergency room, where victims, many of them already dead, initially arrived at the rate of one every eleven seconds. (Courtesy William Noonan, Boston Fire Department)

A truckload of caskets arriving at the Northern Mortuary.

The jury visits the Grove
on March 16, 1943.
(Courtesy William Noonan,
Boston Fire Department)

This is the perspective in the foyer that Ruth Strogoff, Joyce Spector, and others would have seen as they raced the fire up the staircase from the Melody Lounge. The restrooms and checkrooms are on the right, as well as Angelo Lippi's desk. The foyer was the site of the violent explosion and flashover as the superheated gases from the Melody Lounge hit the oxygen-rich room. It was also the first room the jurors saw as they walked in through what had been the revolving-door entrance to the right of the photo. (Courtesy William Noonan, Boston Fire Department)

OPPOSITE PAGE

The jurors would walk first through the burned main entrance to the Grove; the man in the photo is standing in front of the remnants of the revolving door, where bodies were piled eight feet high. The door to the left was the "emergency door" that was locked and blocked on the inside by a coatrack so that Barney could earn "$3.20 a night—there wasn't a penny to be lost," according to Assistant District Attorney Frederick T. Doyle. (Courtesy William Noonan, Boston Fire Department)

The fire started in this corner of the Melody Lounge in the now-demolished palm tree, but the zebra-striped settees, only a few feet away, were largely untouched by fire. (Courtesy William Noonan, Boston Fire Department)

terrace, as seen from the stage. It, too, was intact, although many were trapped on the ace by the metal railing. (Courtesy William Noonan, Boston Fire Department)

OSITE PAGE
ept for the ceiling, the Melody Lounge was remarkably intact, and most who died here ered the effects of smoke inhalation and carbon monoxide poisoning. (Courtesy William nan, Boston Fire Department)

The firefighters removed the inward-swinging door to the New Broadway Lounge. The panicked crowd pressed this door shut. Lieutenant Miles Murphy counted about thirty bodies piled against this door. (Courtesy William Noonan, Boston Fire Department)

Twenty-one-year-old Coastguardsman Clifford Johnson, who suffered through more than 30,000 skin grafts, taking his first steps nearly one year after the fire.

three years." This statement was true enough with regard to his recent stint at the club, but it was not historically accurate. And he answered with emphatic "No sirs" when Reilly asked, "Have you any interest in the Cocoanut Grove financially?" and "No member of your family has any interest . . . ?" Nevertheless, Mickey was not just the Grove's "bandleader"; his association with the establishment had actually pre-dated the Charlie Solomon and Barney Welansky eras. Mickey Alpert had in fact been one of the founders of the Cocoanut Grove fifteen years earlier.

In 1927, Milton Irving Alpert was a restive young man. A recent graduate of Boston University, he had resisted the unanimous opinion of his family that he follow his brother to law school. Mickey had no interest in trailing George, whom everyone agreed was destined for success. (Years later, George Alpert would become the first chairman of Brandeis University, which he was instrumental in founding, and president of the New Haven Railroad. George was also the father of Richard Alpert, also known as Baba Ram Das, the LSD guru of the '60s and '70s.)

The law was too dreary a path for the gregarious Mickey. He dreamt instead of a show business career, which was an odd choice considering his limited talents. Mickey possessed a pleasant but undistinguished voice, a certain knack for light banter, and he looked good in a dinner jacket—modest gifts that seemed unlikely to propel him to stardom. Since graduation, he had picked up a few evening engagements at Boston establishments as leader of the Milton I. Alpert Collegians, but he spent his days languishing in the job brother George had pressured him to take—managing a Newton furniture store.

His friend, Jacob Stavisky, a Boston-area bandleader, rescued him from his ennui. Stavisky, whose professional name was

Jacques Renard, recognized in Mickey a born *tummler*—the Yiddish word for a life-of-the-party, jack-of-all-trades emcee. A journeyman musician, Stavisky and his band had been doing tolerably well playing various Boston and New England venues. But the stubby, bespectacled, multi-chinned violinist was aware of his limitations as a face man, and he enlisted his good-looking pal to do his *shtick* between dance numbers.

One weekend, the Jacques Renard Orchestra, with the versatile Mickey Alpert out front, was engaged at a New Hampshire resort. After one of their shows, the two men learned that they had acquired an ardent fan. They were approached by one Jack Berman, who described himself as a Californian who had something to do with the oil business. He was looking for situations in Boston, he said, and he had a great idea for the two boys. The natty young man explained that he had surveyed Boston nightlife as it existed in 1927 and had found it hopelessly stilted. Boston was ripe for a roaring twenties nightclub, said Berman, and Renard and Alpert were just the guys to put it together. The cigar-chomping, big-spending Berman exuded a can-do attitude, and he impressed the two young men. Berman promised to provide all the financing and to give his new partners full authority.

Mickey consulted his brother George, who was at that time a first assistant district attorney for Suffolk County. George advised his kid brother to proceed cautiously and under no circumstances sell booze. Mickey found a vacant one-story industrial building near the Boston Common and called in club designer Reuben O. Bodenhorn. Bodenhorn mused about a tropical jungle theme for the proposed club, not unlike the already-established Beachcomber. Berman loved the idea and summarily appropriated the Cocoanut Grove name from the nightclub in the Ambassador Hotel in Los Angeles.

Jack Berman proved to be as good as his word. He had only one demand, that everything be "classy." He dug into his seemingly bottomless pockets repeatedly until he had invested a princely sum, rumored to have been as much as $100,000. Berman was, however, strangely reticent about credit. He declined to have his name publicly associated with the Grove and insisted that it be called the Renard Cocoanut Grove. The opening was scheduled for late October 1927, only a few months after Berman had first approached Renard and Alpert at the New Hampshire resort.

However, in September Jack Berman—also known as Jack Bennett, also known as John Roth—surrendered to police in California, where he pleaded not guilty to charges of forgery, embezzlement, conspiracy to obtain money under false pretenses, and conspiracy to violate securities laws. It turned out that during the months when he was playing the financial angel to Renard and Alpert in Boston, he had been a fugitive from these indictments in Los Angeles. There had been reports during this time that he was hiding at his home in New York City or that he had run off to Europe, but he certainly spent enough time in Boston to invest the equivalent of about one million in present-day dollars in the Cocoanut Grove. It turned out that for Berman that was just "spit money," as King Solomon might have observed.

Berman was one of the masterminds of the various Julian Petroleum Corporation swindles in Los Angeles. Julian Petroleum controlled a number of the recently discovered oil fields in and around LA, and because of over-issues of stock and a series of investment pools that lent money to purchase the watered stock at usurious rates, $140,000,000 had been lost by 40,000 investors. At least fifty-five men had been indicted. The scandals swept up such local notables as Louis B. Mayer, founder of MGM, director Cecil B. DeMille, and Harry Haldeman, grandfather of the Watergate conspirator. They were indicted for usury but were cleared or made restitution.

However, Berman was the big fish. Mayer, DeMille, and Haldeman made only thousands. Berman's associates, who were also indicted, accused him of having pocketed $34,000,000 of the company's money. He would ultimately serve seven years in federal prison. Just how many millions Jack Berman stole and kept is unclear, but what is clear is that his enthusiasm for the Cocoanut Grove venture had waned precipitously.

With only weeks to go before the opening, Jacques Renard and Mickey Alpert now found themselves left in the lurch by Berman's abrupt departure, and by the awkwardness of his involvement. Mickey turned to his brother George for advice. What to do about Berman's investment in the Grove? George Alpert brought in attorney John P. Feeney, who happened also to be one of King Solomon's criminal attorneys, and they contacted Jack Berman's lawyers in New York. George and Feeney had one trump card, but it had to be played very carefully. If Berman refused to withdraw, they could inform the Los Angeles authorities of his Boston investment, which had apparently gone undetected. The danger of this stratagem was that the Cocoanut Grove, and with it Renard's and Mickey's dreams, would be entangled in the legal morass of the Julian Petroleum Corporation. After some wrangling and threats, they arrived at a mutually satisfactory solution. Berman would waive all claims to the Grove for $25,000. George Alpert and John Feeney put up $20,000, and Mickey and Jacques came up with the balance.

So the Renard Cocoanut Grove ("The Rendezvous of the Elite") opened on October 27, 1927, with two new, very silent partners, George Alpert and John P. Feeney.

The Renard-Alpert vision was realized. They had created a swanky nightclub, with tuxedoed waiters and a "French" chef—Fred Rousseau, "Boston's Own Famous Restaurateur." Under the supervision of Reuben O. Bodenhorn, a one-story stucco and cement garage in the city's theater and nightclub district had been transformed into an ersatz fantasy "resort," as nightclubs were often described in that era.

For several years, the Grove was successful, with fine food and good shows presided over by the Renard-Alpert team. The "Count" Angelo Lippi was engaged as maître d'. But during an age of speakeasies, the operation was always stifled by the strict no-booze policy dictated by the law-abiding George Alpert. Customers had to bring their own liquor; they paid only for set-ups—ice, glasses, and mixers—an inconvenience for them and not very lucrative for the club. Then came the Depression.

By 1930 business was floundering. To make matters worse, Jacques Renard bolted, joining "Berkie" Kravitz at his new enterprise, the Mayfair, just around the corner on Broadway. Kravitz, a bootlegger, naturally had no compunctions about serving alcohol.

It was at this point that King Solomon stepped in to buy the Grove from the partners. Barney Welansky handled the negotiations. Welansky contacted George Alpert and put to him Solomon's proposition, reputed to be a mere $10,000—a tenth of what Berman had invested and less than half what George and Feeny had put in. Nevertheless, the partners jumped at the offer. Mickey remained as majordomo for two years after the sale, but then decided that he didn't share the King's style and moved on from what by now had become an all-out speakeasy, albeit a classy one.

The King reigned at the Grove until his rubout in 1933, when Barney came into his "inheritance."

Among the first decisions Barney had made after taking over was to cut back the costs of the shows. Charlie Solomon, always cultivating his impresario image, had paraded the 1930's biggest nightclub acts across the Grove's stage. Jimmy Durante, Rudy Vallee, and Guy Lombardo performed during the King's short tenure. Sophie Tucker, "the last of the red-hot mommas," was a regular headliner. Another big voice, Belle Baker, appeared at the Grove not long after introducing Irving Berlin's "Blue Skies" on Broadway. Helen Morgan, who draped herself atop the piano for her throaty signature song, "My Bill," appeared shortly after her success in the new Broadway musical, *Show Boat*. Mary Louise "Texas" Guinan performed with her all-girl band and was paid by Solomon what was reputed at the time to be the highest weekly salary for any nightclub act in the country. Guinan, a speakeasy owner in her own right in New York, greeted the Grove crowd with her trademark "hello suckers" salutation.

The King had also engaged another group of stars whose radiance faded along with their figures, but whose names were recalled after the fire by the *Boston American*: Francie Williams, who "contorted her terrific torso," Ann Pennington, "who jiggled her meaty thorax," and Gilda Gray, "who had shimmied her supple and seductive body into fame in the Ziegfeld Follies."

This big-name policy ended abruptly with Barney. He trimmed the entertainment back to salaried house bands, an Irish tenor—Billy Payne—a dance team, an occasional violinist, and chorus boys and girls. In 1939, he re-hired the amiable Mickey Alpert to be the club's entertainment producer and emcee, roles that Welansky had no interest in or aptitude for. While Mickey was billed as the "leader" of the orchestra, saxophonist Bernie Fazioli, who was killed in the fire, had actually been in charge of the musicians.

And so, by 1942, Barney had slashed his entertainment budget while nearly tripling the size of his nightclub. The shows were reliably popular, but much cheaper to stage than they had been during the profligate Solomon era. Furthermore, under his guidance, the Grove had grown to about nine hundred seats, and Barney now employed about one hundred people.

Barney's predecessors had been bad businessmen. Mickey had been chasing his dreams, and Solomon his ego. Barney, however, was clear-eyed and determined. Surely, unlike his ill-fated predecessors, he had at last brought the Grove under his firm and watchful control. The outwardly brilliant nightspot that had been born under such dubious circumstances had brought the previous owners only gloom. Now the man who would be its final owner, the poor boy from the West End who had struggled his entire life, must have believed that his quest was over, the Grove having finally brought him respect, influence, and wealth.

But it had literally gone up in smoke.

CHAPTER 9

The Man Who
Wasn't There

[Barney was there] every night. . . . His word was everything. . . . He was the owner, the actual owner and manager. . . . His word was the say at the Cocoanut Grove.

Mickey Alpert

NO ONE KNOWS WHEN Barney got the bad news. By early
Sunday morning, Massachusetts General Hospital—his
residence for the previous thirteen days—had taken in 114 victims of the fire. But Welansky may not have been aware of the
turmoil at the hospital's White Building, where all of the Grove
victims were being treated. He was in a separate building, the
more serene, high-end Phillips House.

Even so, Barney surely learned by Sunday morning that his
physical ailments were the least of his troubles. His brother
Jimmy and Herbert F. Callahan, his law partner and the man
who would become his chief strategist and defender, must have
been among the bearers of the bad news. One can only imagine
how Barney's sense of horror over the deaths must have been
tempered by his instinct for self-preservation.

Perhaps at that moment he recalled the letter written to him in 1939 by an advertising man who had handled the Grove's publicity. The letter had warned: "Your exits are very bad. You've got tinderbox construction. It should be in absolute conformity with the building rules." What's more, Barney, Jimmy, and Callahan may have discussed how they would deal with the characteristically uneventful "inspection" on November 20 by the Fire Prevention Bureau's Frank Linney, after which the lieutenant had reported "no inflammable decoration" and a "sufficient number of exits." And what about those fusible doors that were supposed to be installed in the corridor to the New Broadway Lounge? Theodore Eldracher, the building department inspector who was to have signed off on their installation before the room opened, had quietly dropped the matter. Had Jimmy taken care of these municipal functionaries with a few bucks and a few drinks, or had they simply deferred to the well-connected Welanskys?

Who would they hold responsible for all of this—for the flammable satin that had carried the fire up the staircase and into the main dining room, for the 1,000 people in a room licensed for 460, for the locked exit doors? Young Stanley Tomaszewski would give a good account of himself, and most citizens were sympathetic to the boy. The politicians would no doubt obscure their responsibility.

Whatever corrupt and incompetent public officials had or had not done, their inaction would provide a flimsy shield for Barney. He must have known that the politicians would run for the hills and that he would be left holding the bag. After all, Barney *was* the Grove. Ignorance was no excuse, and ignorance was not his only sin. He surely must have felt the noose beginning to tighten the moment he learned of the fire.

Barney Welansky's personal journey had been in so many ways the classic American story of the child of immigrants who had steadily climbed the ladder of success through personal discipline, hard work, and education. As an earnest teenager, he sold newspapers in downtown Boston and so impressed his superiors that he was rewarded with a plum distributorship at the corner of Mass Avenue and Boylston Street. He went on to earn both a bachelor's and a master's law degree from Boston University by the age of twenty-one. After that, things got even better. He had become the law partner of Herbert F. Callahan, said to be one of Boston's best criminal lawyers, and of course, the owner of the city's pre-eminent nightclub.

Nevertheless, despite these accomplishments, and his wealth, Barney seemed possessed by a lingering insecurity that probably generated his boast to his hireling, Henry Weene, that "Tobin and I fit. They owe me plenty." This loser's boast could close the case against him in the public mind. But that remark was only Exhibit A in the case against him. Given the lax rules of evidence for trying a case in the press, he knew he was in deep trouble.

Barney's friend and mentor, Herbert F. Callahan, must have gone to work right away. He likely contacted all of his and Barney's political connections, including the mayor and the fire commissioner, to remind them of Barney's friendship. He no doubt had a fruitful conversation with the police commissioner, Joseph F. Timilty, or someone else among the police brass, which paid off immediately.

On Sunday afternoon, the Boston police had found the Grove's financial and business records among the embers. They were then taken to the Warren Avenue police station. The next day, on November 30, the records mysteriously wound up in

Callahan's Pemberton Square office. It would be two days before they were returned to the police. Bushnell's people then promptly snatched them for safekeeping from the Boston police, but no one would ever learn what Callahan had done to the records. More significantly, no one would ever ask.

Barney would not be discharged from Massachusetts General Hospital until December 11, nearly two weeks after the fire. Upon his release, his physician, Dr. Harry B. Levine, sent a letter to Reilly, supported by the examination of the renowned cardiologist Dr. Paul Dudley White, informing the fire commissioner that Barney would be unable to undergo the rigors of testimony for at least three weeks after his release. The timing was convenient for Barney since the term of the grand jury before which Bushnell was presenting evidence expired on December 31. He would never testify before Reilly or Bushnell's grand jury. But public resentment was already building, as evidenced by an anonymous letter to Dr. Levine accusing him of complicity in a cover-up: "Too bad there are doctors like you who care so little for lives. What about the hundreds who sleep in the dust? Welansky should answer now, and I feel you should answer too, for lying."

Despite his doctor's opinion that he was still in poor health, Barney had nevertheless been able to do some business from his hospital bed. On December 8, he executed two leases with Albert, Mary Amelia, and Frederick Eichorn covering the three small buildings that constituted the storage rooms attached to the New Broadway Lounge, buildings Barney did not own. The leases, dated August 1942, but signed and recorded *after* the fire, stated explicitly that the tenant—Barney—bore sole responsibility for damage and injury resulting from fire. Why would Barney have agreed to the assumption of responsibility from the Eichorns? This confusing after-the-fact lease arrangement reinforced the common opinion that Barney was the master of undocumented and convoluted business arrangements, just like his mysterious "inheritance" of the Grove.

But beyond the questions raised by such puzzling relationships, the pressure on Barney escalated as Boston's press quickly moved from the inevitable first-day overview descriptions to stories of personal tragedies.

The heart-wrenching stories included the four Fitzgerald brothers—James, Wilfred, Henry, and John. The brothers died with their dates at a Grove furlough party for Henry, a private in the Army Air Corps. Henry, who was stationed in Florida, hadn't been home for more than six months. "They didn't go to the Cocoanut Grove just to be at a nightclub," said their seventy-one-year-old mother Mary, but to show "Henry that they were really glad to see him again. The other boys were like kids when they saw him again."

They had gone with their dates to the BC–Holy Cross game and then to the Grove "to have some fun," said Mrs. Fitzgerald. Her husband had died twenty years earlier, leaving Mrs. Fitzgerald with a house full of children. "They said they always wanted to be with me forever. I was their girl, they told me," she said in her now-still house.

Three of the brothers were found immediately. John was missing for a full day after the fire. "I know he's dead too," said the heartbroken mother. Mrs. Fitzgerald was right. "They were fine boys. I don't know whether I can stand it or not," she said.

There were two hundred military uniform caps found in the Grove checkroom. This and other reports, such as the loss of the

Fitzgerald brothers, underscored the relative youth of most of the victims—soldiers, sailors, college kids, young couples. Perhaps half of the victims were under thirty-five, many in their late teens and early twenties. Fifty-five servicemen died in the fire.

On December 1, 52 victims were buried; on December 2, there were more than 100 funerals for Grove victims; on December 3, there were 150 funerals. Many of these were multiple funerals for husbands and wives or siblings. At least eleven children from five families lost both their parents. The papers were filled with stories such as the funerals for Edward McCarthy and his wife, Eileen, parents of the now orphaned Jane Frances, five years old, and Edward Jr., three months old.*

Four caskets faced the altar of the Holy Trinity Church in the South End four days after the fire. They were the caskets of Lawrence Kenny, the Boston College athletic director, his wife, Maria Theresa, and her brother and sister-in-law. Larry's brother, Father Charles Kenny, celebrated the high mass of requiem. Members of the BC football team were the pallbearers.

The papers featured pictures and stories of seemingly endless lines of people outside of the Northern and Southern Mortuaries, as well as the garages near the Grove that were used as temporary morgues. The stories described grief-stricken relatives and friends threading their way through the rows of the dead and the occasional screams of denial that attended a dreaded identification.

---

*These tragedies became so indelible that the *Boston Globe*'s April 29, 2000, obituary for Norinne (Feeny) Walsh noted that she had "raised seven children as well as three nieces and nephews after their parents perished in the Cocoanut Grove fire in 1942. She was 89." Timothy and Margaret Feeny died at the Grove along with Margaret's brother, William Young. Young was scheduled to enter the U.S. Navy the next morning, and the group was at the Grove for a send-off party.

Boston Police Lieutenant John J. Gale was one of those on this gloomy trek. Lieutenant Gale spent two days and nights searching the city's hospitals and morgues for his son Francis. The search ended sadly at Boston City Hospital, were Dr. Albert Murphy identified the young Gale's otherwise unidentifiable body from an appendectomy scar, the result of an operation he had performed several months earlier with Dr. Gordon Bennett, who had himself died as a result of burns sustained at the Grove.

Lynn Andrews, the Grove's photographer, was an unwitting chronicler of the heartbreak. She had slipped her fur coat over her thin evening dress and left the club at about 9:30 P.M. to walk to her Church Street studio where she developed the pictures she had taken. She planned to return to the Grove in time to collect the one-dollar per picture fee from her subjects. Barney forbade picture-taking or other distractions during the floor show, so Lynn had left in time to get back with the prints before the show was to begin. Instead, she got back to the Grove just in time to see it in flames. Shortly, she would learn that most of the subjects in her pictures were dead. During the next week, Lynn's photographic records of so many last moments of life would be front-page features.

One of the pictures Lynn had developed, the one with reference number "4" in the lower left-hand corner, was of a very happy young couple seated at a table, their arms around each other in loving embrace. The couple who were the subject of the picture had wanted to leave, but they agreed to wait until Lynn got back with the print. The woman was wearing an enormous corsage that ran from her breast over her shoulder. The man had a carnation pinned to his lapel.

Until seven o'clock that evening, the woman's name had been Claudia Nadeau. By the time the picture was taken, she was Mrs. John O'Neil. The North Cambridge couple had been married that evening at Notre Dame de Pitie Church and were celebrating at the Grove with their best man and bridesmaid, John Doyle and Ann Rita O'Neil, the bridegroom's sister. Claudia's brother had dropped off the wedding party at the Latin Quarter on nearby Winchester Street, and no one knew why or when they had moved from there to the Grove.

The O'Neils' married life together lasted a little more than three hours. On Wednesday, December 2, after funeral masses in Cambridge, the O'Neils and their best man and bridesmaid were laid to rest.

Some newspapers reported that half a million people wandered past what was left of the Grove on Sunday. The steady stream of onlookers had begun gathering the night before—some no doubt just curious, others perhaps searching for friends and family. Martial law had been declared at 1:35 A.M. to control the crowd, but there was no problem maintaining order. It was a quiet group, and it moved mostly in stunned silence. They had come to see the eerie remains of the fabulous "Rendezvous of the Elite."

During the next weeks, there would be a cascade of "revelations" about Barney, his brother Jimmy, and their "connections." Although a few of these disclosures were relevant to the question of his responsibility, most were only curiosities. But they all contributed to the developing picture of a shady character.

In addition to his personal image problems, Barney had to bear the albatross of his tough little brother Jimmy. Besides noting that Jimmy had operated the Theatrical Club speakeasy during Prohibition, the Boston papers recalled that in 1938 Jimmy had been a material witness in the investigation into the murder of Daniel "Beano" Breen. He and Beano had been partners in a gambling operation at the Nantasket Beach recreation center. Something had gone awry, and Jimmy was left holding the bag for a $20,000 loss.

Shortly thereafter, Beano was shot to death in the lobby of the Metropolitan Hotel, which was managed by Jimmy. Jimmy admitted being in the lobby but claimed that a mysterious assassin, whom he could not describe, had done the deed. A judge hearing the preliminary evidence concluded, however, that the "assassin" was "a theatrical apparition." The judge charged, "It is apparent that there is only one person who could have shot Breen." Inexplicably, however, no indictment was handed down by the grand jury. Although he was never charged with the crime, Jimmy remained a material witness and technically subject to being recalled in the investigation. He was out on bail, which had been posted by Katherine Welch, a secretary in the law office of Barney's pal and partner, Herbert F. Callahan. Katherine Welch's name would crop up in a number of different settings.

A few days after the fire, Jimmy testified before Reilly's investigation. Since he had only been filling in for his sick brother, said Jimmy, he knew next to nothing about the operations of the Grove, its decorations or its exits. Every "I don't know" or "I couldn't say" answer smacked of a cover-up. In addition, Jimmy's vague description that he "presumed" that he was carried by the crowd out of the Grove—Captain Buccigross had testified that "[Jimmy] Welansky left at once"—did little to help the family image. Then in mid-December, Attorney General

Bushnell called him before the grand jury. By this time, no doubt realizing that the noose was closing on him as well as Barney, Jimmy invoked his Fifth Amendment right not to testify against himself.

Nevertheless, Jimmy had already done damage to the Welanskys' cause. In addition to his barrage of "I don't know"s about the club, Jimmy had inadvertently hurt his older brother by answering a question about the seating capacity of the club. Evidently unaware that Barney had represented the seating capacity of the Grove to be about 460, Jimmy said, "I would say that it would hold about 900."

Then there were Jimmy's maneuverings on November 17, the day of the opening of the New Broadway Lounge. Back in August, an official of the state Alcoholic Beverage Commission (ABC) had reviewed the plans for the New Broadway Lounge with Barney and a licensing board representative. The ABC official told them that there was a problem with the proposed layout. A door at the end of the passageway leading to the new room would interrupt the continuity of the premises and therefore a new and independent license would be required. A new license might be a problem. In addition to taking more time, it raised the issue of separate but abutting establishments serving liquor. The quick-thinking Barney had assured the ABC man this door would always be open, except in emergencies. It was to be a fusible door, he said; it would close automatically only if there was a fire.

On the morning of the opening, Miss Mary E. Driscoll, who had been on the Boston licensing board for nearly eighteen years, and now nearly three years as chair, read the newspaper advertisements announcing the opening:

THE LUXURIOUS AND BREATH-TAKING CO-
COANUT GROVE LOUNGE, BEAUTIFULLY DECO-
RATED AND COMFORTABLY ARRANGED TO PLEASE
EVEN THE MOST FASTIDIOUS.

Miss Driscoll instructed one of her clerks to call the Grove
and gently remind the management that the nightclub's liquor
license extension for the new lounge had not received final
approval.

Jimmy took the call in Barney's absence. As nimble as his
brother, Jimmy assured the clerk that all was in order, implying
that the fusible fire doors had been installed and that there was
a fire exit in the New Broadway Lounge. Of course, there were
no fusible doors and the "fire exit" was blocked by a checkroom
that Barney had installed as an afterthought. Jimmy also ne-
glected to mention that there had been no final inspection and
sign-off by the building department. The department's inspector, Theodore Eldracher, had quietly dropped the matter. Nevertheless, shortly before the licensing board closed for the day,
at just about 5 P.M. of opening night, the accommodating Miss
Driscoll signed the license extension and handed it to Jimmy.
The New Broadway Lounge opened as planned solely upon
Jimmy's glib assurance that all was "according to Hoyle."

The name Katherine Welch, Callahan's secretary, who had
posted bond for Jimmy in connection with the Beano Breen
murder, also showed up in the corporate papers for the Cocoanut Grove. In 1942, Barney was president of the corporation. Katherine Welch and Welansky's sister, Jennie, were the
other officers. The corporation held no meetings and had no
minutes, and Welch and Jennie told Reilly that they could
shed no light on its operations. Jennie told Reilly that she had

only visited the Grove for an occasional dinner but that she worked as the bookkeeper for another nightspot, the Rio Casino. This was a nearby club behind the Hotel Bradford ostensibly owned by a man named Al Taxier, who had himself been summoned to testify by Attorney General Bushnell. Adding to the picture of intriguing interlocks, Katherine Welch told Reilly that she was also a director of the corporation that owned the Rio Casino as well as of the Circle Lounge Bar in Brighton, owned by Jimmy Welansky.*

There was nothing unusual, then or now, about closely held corporations not being run by the book; nor was there anything unusual about a lawyer's secretary being a nominal director—a "straw" or "dummy" officer—of a small corporation. Jennie and Ms. Welch were classic dummy shareholder-directors. Barney had retained Ms. Welch's and his sister's stock certificates, which he had them endorse in blank so that he could insert his name later if necessary. These were just Barney's shortcuts, but a picture was emerging of a man who turned shortcuts into tangled, impenetrable webs.

Take, for instance, the 1934 lawsuit brought by the Isaac Locke Company. The provisions firm had done business with Charlie Solomon and sued Barney's New Cocoanut Grove Inc. to collect an unpaid bill for $248.52. However, the plaintiff's problem was more complicated than simply proving that steaks, roasts, and hamburger had been supplied and not paid for. The Locke Company had dealt with a company that no longer existed, and the successor entity had lost its assets.

---

*Many of the Grove employees had assembled at the Rio Casino after the fire, apparently on Jimmy's instructions.

In October of 1933—the King had been murdered in January—Barney had transferred the Grove's real estate to the *New* Cocoanut Grove Inc., whose officers were the ubiquitous Katherine Welch, maître d' Angelo Lippi, and Barney. (During the entire time Charlie Solomon was the owner of the Grove, his name never appeared on corporate papers. Instead, Angelo Lippi was listed as a director and treasurer. Angelo later explained that Barney and the King had set it up that way. His sole duty as treasurer, Lippi recalled, was to sign wads of blank checks whenever the King told him to.)

The Locke complaint stated that the New Cocoanut Grove Inc. had given a $5,500 mortgage on the Grove's real estate to none other than Barney. Barney explained in his own court papers that he had taken the mortgage back to secure periodic cash payments he had made to the new corporation so that it could carry on its business. Sadly, however, Barney's corporation could not make any payments to Barney and he foreclosed on his own corporation. The real estate was then sold at a foreclosure sale—to his sister Jennie. "I believe the amount was $3,000," Barney explained about the price he had paid. The effect of the foreclosure was that there was no property in the corporate name on which the Locke Company or other creditors could execute a judgment.

The Locke Company charged that the re-incorporation had been a scam to stiff creditors, that the mortgage was phony, and that the foreclosure and sale were conducted "with the intent to delay, defeat or defraud" creditors so that Welansky could "secure the property for himself without paying fair consideration." Barney wisely settled the case before it proceeded further, and the lawsuit would have remained an obscure collection action had it not been for the fire and Barney's unwelcome notoriety.

Rose Gnecco, formerly Rose Gnecco Ponzi, the corporation's bookkeeper, brought Barney notoriety of a different sort. Ms. Gnecco was the divorced wife of Charles Ponzi, the swindler whose name has become an eponym for pyramid schemes.

In 1919, Charles Ponzi devised a scheme for borrowing small sums of money from individuals, promising them a 50 percent return on their loans. He claimed that the loans were to be used to finance an arcane "international postal coupon redemption" operation. In fact, Ponzi's only business had been serial borrowing. He would borrow $100 from lender 1. Ponzi then used the $200 he got from lenders 2 and 3 to repay lender 1 his $150, pocketing the extra $50. Then he would borrow from lenders 4, 5, 6, and 7, rake off $100 more, and then repay lenders 2 and 3 $150 apiece, and on and on. By 1920, Ponzi had collected almost $10 million from about 10,000 individuals. Obviously, since the scheme required an ever-expanding pool of lenders, his luck eventually ran out. Ponzi was deported to his native Italy in 1934, after having served nine years in prison.

While none of this had ever touched Rose, the vicarious Ponzi connection added to the general sense of disrepute surrounding Barney. Rose, understandably, had long-since dropped the Ponzi name, but the Boston press insisted on reverting to her married name.

The once beautiful but now bespectacled, matronly Rose had been the Grove's bookkeeper since the King Solomon days. She testified that Barney had arranged for the Grove receipts—or some of them at least—to be regularly deposited into a special account in her name at the Pilgrim Trust Company, simply as a matter of "convenience."

Reilly asked Rose, "Did you pay the help at the Cocoanut Grove?"

"Yes," she replied.

"Was this money from a checking account?"

"Yes."

"In effect, your personal account?"

"Yes."

In addition, Mrs. Gnecco testified that Barney had purchased large quantities of liquor in anticipation of shortages and price increases. In other words, Barney was hoarding, an unpatriotic act in wartime. Sure enough, within days after the fire, thousands of cases of bottled liquors—without federal tax stamps—were discovered below trapdoors in bricked-lined caverns under the Grove. Moreover, a fireman had privately reported to Chief Pope that "one of the skylights on the Piedmont Street side [over the Caricature Bar] was blocked off and loaded with cases of liquor hidden away." The implication was clear: Barney had protected the liquor but not his customers.

Barney was also the recipient of inordinate city largesse. For instance, Daniel M. Driscoll, head of the city department in charge of tax-foreclosed property, acknowledged that his department had arranged for Barney to purchase the building that became part of the New Broadway Lounge. The building, which had been seized by the city for nonpayment of taxes, had been sold to Jennie Welansky—standing in for Barney—"at public auction" in 1940 for $6,000, a price set by "a committee of real estate men." Just how "public" was this "auction"? "We thought the Cocoanut Grove people, who were the abutters, were the most logical purchasers, so I contacted them," explained Driscoll. At the time of the sale to Jennie, the city's assessment for tax purposes was $13,000; it was reduced to $10,000 in 1941 and then dropped to $9,000 in 1942.

Then it was revealed by investigators at the ostensibly secret Bushnell inquiry that in 1941 Barney had also secured a $10,000 reduction in the valuation of the principal Grove property at 17 Piedmont Street. Edward T. Kelly, chairman of the Boston Board of Assessors, testified that the board's "street man," who had "conferred with a member of the board," had proposed the reduction. After this "conference," which was the "customary procedure" according to Kelly, the Grove valuation was reduced from $70,000 to $60,000 during a year of an improving economy.

Concerned that Barney might skip town, the state police were patrolling the halls of the Phillips House at Massachusetts General Hospital during his stay. After his release, the police kept a watchful eye on his apartment at 1691 Commonwealth Avenue in the Brighton section of the city.

Throughout the month, the drama was building. There was speculation about the impending indictments. There were rumors about politicians, contractors, and workmen and even about some Grove employees.

But there was never any doubt about Barney Welansky.

CHAPTER 10

The Bright Side?

Fire kills in several ways.

Dr. Francis D. Moore

BY ALL MEDICAL RECKONING, Clifford Johnson was as good as dead by about 10:45 P.M.

Like so many other young men at the Grove that evening, Clifford was a long way from home. The tall, slender twenty-one-year-old Coast Guardsman with a Jimmy Stewart–like demeanor from rural Missouri was stationed in Nahant, about nine miles north of Boston. He and his buddy Harold Davis had come down from the Coast Guard station for weekend leave. That afternoon Harold's date had introduced Clifford to Estelle Balkan. Clifford and Estelle were in the New Broadway Lounge with Harold and his girl when the flames roared through. The momentum of the frantic crowd carried Clifford safely through the door on to Broadway, but Estelle's hand had slipped from his grasp, and she was trapped inside. Clifford turned around and plunged back into the fire four times in a gallant but futile effort to save his new friend. He never found the girl, but he reportedly helped several others to escape.

143

Clifford had bucked the odds and lost. He emerged from his last attempt a ball of flame and fell on the sidewalk.

He was still alive when he arrived at Boston City Hospital, but just barely. Everyone was certain that he would die within hours. He had suffered third-degree burns over about half of his body and second-degree burns over another quarter. In 1942, no one had ever survived such extensive deep dermal burns.

Large areas of Clifford's flesh were burned away, completely exposing parts of his ribs, the bone above one knee, and a part of his jawbone. His back—from his neck to his ankles—was a mass of white, red, black, yellow, and brown crusts wherever the fire had burned through the outer and inner layers of skin down to, and in some places through, the subcutaneous fat. The doctors could see his right kidney.

Remarkably, unlike the majority of victims, Clifford had suffered little lung or airway damage, but that was the only good news. His breathing was shallow, his pulse weak, his temperature below normal—and he was losing fluids. Boston City physicians were certain that Clifford would soon suffer the inexorable sequence of bodily reactions that was then the fate of all victims with such severe burns—leaking, infection, shock, death.

Nevertheless, this sturdy farm boy's body seemed determined not to die, and the medical staff worked heroically to keep him alive. They pumped him with fluids, fed him intravenously, administered antibiotics, and tended to his wounds.

In treating his wounds, Clifford's doctors employed a procedure that gave resonance to the cliché about the cure being worse than the disease.

The penetration of heat deep into the skin leaves a layer of decomposed epidermis and dermis—burn eschar. The bubbling, necrotic "soup" formed by the dead eschar and the subcutaneous fatty tissue is the ideal culture for bacterial, fungal, and viral infections emanating from the body itself as well as the environment. Physicians at Boston City employed the standard "tanning" process to fight this infection and leaking at the burn sites. First, Clifford was shot up with morphine to kill the pain of his burns—and of the treatment. Then he was "debrided."

In 1942, debridement entailed scrubbing the wound and picking at it to remove debris and dead skin. First, pieces of clothing, cinders, and other foreign material were scrubbed at and pulled away. Then the *blebs*—blisters—were popped and, finally, the burned and dead skin was sliced off all the way down to the remaining healthy tissue. The wounds were treated with antibacterial agents, such as tannic acid, and then slathered with greenish/purple-colored "triple dyes." Just as tanning turns soft animal hide to leather, the purpose of this "tanning" was to cause the formation of a leathery scab to shield against infection and further loss of fluids.

The initial treatment consumed many hours, but this was not a one-time procedure. Clifford's wounds were examined daily in a determined search for infection; the wounds were repeatedly re-cleaned and re-scraped as deemed necessary. To ease the constant pain, the doctors administered codeine instead of the more addictive morphine. Because of the severity and extent of the damage, Clifford's wounds were not completely bandaged. He kept leaking, and each day his bed sheets were stained a ghastly purple color from the mixture of dripping body fluids and the triple dyes.

Dr. Oliver Cope was convinced that there was a better approach to treatment. At the time of the Grove fire, Cope was the man in charge of treating burns at Massachusetts General

Hospital. Though only forty years old, Cope was a highly respected surgeon at the hospital. By the time he was in his early thirties, Cope had already distinguished himself as a surgical endocrinologist. After Pearl Harbor, Cope turned to the challenge of surgical treatment of burn patients. Not a man to take received knowledge uncritically, Cope was convinced that the standard treatment being used at Boston City Hospital and all other hospitals gave undo attention to the burn site. Although he understood that debridement was a necessary preparation for skin grafting, Cope was convinced that it should not be part of the initial treatment protocol.

Cope believed that the leaking through the burn wound was only the most obvious loss of bodily fluids. Forty years after the Grove fire, he recalled the tanning method that he had observed as a young physician years before the Grove fire: "I remember one [burn victim] most vividly . . . there was a man in the bathtub. An intern and a nurse were debriding him, taking off the blebs [blisters], and the nurse was pouring tannic acid on him. I came back a little later and he had died—no fluid. All of the attention was on the burn wound."

By 1942, Dr. Cope had come to believe that the conventional approach to burn treatment was misguided. He was convinced that undue immediate attention to the burn site was needlessly labor intensive and time consuming. As a result, overburdened doctors tended to ignore, or at least to undertreat, the risk of shock. Furthermore, he also believed that the fluid within the blister of second-degree burns was sterile and therefore better protection than tannic acid and triple dyes, substances that he believed retarded healing.

Years later, Dr. Cope told a story about a very small-scale experiment he had conducted on his three-year-old niece in 1935. One day, he received a frantic telephone call from his sister. Her daughter had spilled a hot pot of coffee on herself and had suffered second-degree burns to her hand and wrist. Cope drove to his sister's house with a large pot of Vaseline and sterile bandages. When he arrived, he saw that the child had developed blisters over the burned areas. The standard treatment would have required popping those blisters and cleaning the wound. Cope described what he did instead: "I piled the grease on and put on a . . . bandage and left."

Such minimal treatment of a moderately severe burn concerned Cope's colleagues at Mass General, not least the little girl's father, Cope's brother-in-law and an important member of the staff. Against all the conventional wisdom, Cope insisted on leaving the little girl alone and allowing the burns to heal without scraping or cleaning them. He recalled that when the bandage was removed from his little niece, "you couldn't tell which hand was burned."

Dr. Cope very plausibly argued that the standard procedure for treating the burn area, with its constant manipulation of the patient and the sheer pain of the process, increased the likelihood of shock. Working under a federal grant from the Office of Scientific Research, Cope had in the months before the fire observed the wounds of twenty-six burn patients who had not been debrided and concluded, "The healing beneath the unruptured blebs occurred as rapidly as under any of the agents commonly recommended." On the night of the fire, he unhesitatingly ordered that a new protocol be employed.

The burn surfaces of the victims taken to Mass General were not cleaned or debrided. In an article in *Annals of Surgery* in 1943, Dr. Cope described the injuries presented by the Grove victims and the procedure adopted:

> The burns were sooty and shaggy, with unruptured blebs. Many [patients] were a cherry-red color from carbon monoxide poisoning. Some of them looked clean, others grossly dirty. Many of the patients had been crawling on the floor at the fire, others had been dragged out from piles of the dead. . . . Some of the unconscious who had lived had been incontinent of both urine and feces.
>
> [Only] one type of surface treatment was applied to the burns of the skin of all of the 39 patients. A bland ointment with protective dressing was applied without any preliminary debridement or cleansing, and antibacterial chemotherapy was given internally.

The wounds, together with the dead skin, filth, and detritus, were covered with gauze saturated with boric ointment—essentially Vaseline—and the bandage left undisturbed for a minimum of five days, often longer. Pressure bandages were placed over the gauze to reduce leakage. Antibacterial sulfa drugs were administered orally or by injection.* Weeks later, when the patient was stronger and more tolerant to pain, the most serious wounds could finally be debrided in preparation for skin grafting.

---

*Some penicillin was used. The victims at Mass General were the first to be generally administered the drug, which had been developed only seven years earlier. Later, when the new drug was better understood, it was determined that the dosages administered were too small to be effective.

Cope vigorously defended his radical approach in his 1943 article: "The increased manipulation of the patient, prolonged exposure of the wounds, and anesthetics attendant to debridement are conducive to serious shock." This was, he maintained, "first aid and definitive treatment combined." In other words, this was first aid to minimize the risk of shock as well as the first step toward longer-term treatment.

But what is "shock"?

Everyone has been burned, and for the vast majority the experience is a minor, localized, and temporary irritation. Common match burns or sunburns result in little more than the reddening of the skin or perhaps the stinging of a small blister.

A major burn has quite different consequences. Unlike the injury to a small portion of the body's surface that everyone has experienced, a deep dermal burn is perhaps the most serious trauma the body can suffer. Moreover, the burn site itself is the least important problem, as the trauma caused by the burn extends well beyond the burn site to assault the entire body in a maddeningly reinforcing succession of physiological responses that threaten virtually every major organ. It all begins with a reduction in the volume of blood flowing through the body.

By a process that is still not completely understood, a major burn generates an inflammatory response in which the body releases chemicals that cause some fluids in blood vessels to leak into the surrounding tissues and the vessels themselves to expand. Widened blood vessels are now carrying a thickened and reduced volume of blood, resulting in the loss of blood pressure.

This reduction in blood volume and flow, called hypovolemia, has the same effect as a heart attack. During a heart attack, the blood volume is adequate, but the heart's pumping action is insufficient to sustain the body's tissues. In hypo-volemic shock, the heart's pumping action may be adequate but cannot compensate for the reduction in blood volume. In both cases, the effect is identical. Deprived of oxygen and biochemical exchange—the carrying away of carbon dioxide and tissue waste that would normally be processed by the liver or kidneys or expelled through the lungs—the body's cells die.

The leaking of blood vessels that leads to hypovolemia is also doing mischief at the burn site itself. The leakage accumulates in the skin and tissue surrounding the wound, causing swelling—edema. Edema can physically block the flow of blood through veins and arteries, further reducing blood pressure, oxygen replenishment, and cleansing of body tissue.

The immense loss of body fluids and body heat through the severely burned skin can double, triple, or quadruple the body's rate of metabolism. With the body operating in high gear, nutritional requirements are dramatically increased. An average-size person will need a daily intake of many thousands of additional calories over the normal requirement of 2,000–2,500 calories. This burn-induced malnutrition, among other things, causes further weakness in the body's immune system, which is already challenged by infection from the burn site. Unfortunately, the process of intravenous feeding can also cause swelling of the body's organs and further impairment of their function.

The victim who survives the threat of hypovolemic shock over the first hours or days may nevertheless slip into another, even more deadly form of shock. During the early stages of burn treatment, victims may present the symptoms that Clifford Johnson did—shallow breathing and a drop in body temperature and pulse rate. Then the turnaround begins. The patient develops a high temperature, and the heart begins to beat at a dangerously rapid pace. These are signs that the lungs or the gastrointestinal system have released toxins that have invaded the bloodstream. The infection is spreading.

Unless checked, infection over a large area of the body leads to the condition commonly referred to as blood poisoning— sepsis or septicemia. Sepsis is an "all of the above" condition, a toxic rampage against the lungs, brain, liver, kidneys, heart, stomach, intestines, and blood vessels. The liver, for instance, gradually loses its ability to manufacture needed body chemicals, which in turn further impairs the body's immune system and its ability to fight infection. Less blood flowing to the kidneys means less blood being filtered and a further buildup of toxins in the bloodstream. Along the way, brain function is impaired, and the linings of the stomach and intestines ulcerate and bleed. The cycle of poisoned, oxygen-starved blood in ever reducing volume builds on itself and, one by one, the organs die.

Clifford Johnson indeed suffered the deadly synergy that accompanies deep dermal burns—loss of bodily fluids, edema, oxygen starvation, reduction of blood volume, infection from the burn or from the body's inability to cleanse itself, and malnutrition. And his dedicated surgeon, Dr. Newton Browder, had administered an astounding 30,000 pinprick skin grafts. Years later, Dr. Stanley Levenson, who had been a young researcher at Boston City Hospital at the time of the fire, remembered, "Dr. Browder did thousands of pinpoint skin grafts moving bits of Johnson's skin from uninjured areas to wounds, all of them, as I recall, with a Gillette blue blade." For long periods after these grafts, Clifford would have to lie immobile on his belly, while he and the doctors waited for the thousands of little pieces of skin to grow together on his back.

Then, just as his doctors came to believe that they had turned the corner and that Johnson would recover, they faced a series of setbacks.

At one point, thousands of small grafts onto Clifford's back— the grafts that had taken so many hours to apply—had sloughed off. They would all have to be re-done. More healthy skin would be removed, and there would be more blood loss, pain, risk of infection, and general trauma.

This depressing news pushed Clifford to the edge, according to one commentator. Paul Benzaquin recounts in his book that Harold Davis visited with Clifford shortly after he learned that he had lost the grafts.* Davis was the fellow Coast Guardsman who had been in the New Broadway Lounge with Clifford and Estelle. Davis and his date had escaped with minor injuries. According to Benzaquin's account of Harold's visit, the profoundly depressed Clifford said to his friend, "I want you to bring me a loaded gun." Davis refused and kept secret his friend's chilling request.

Benzaquin also relates another demon stalking Clifford: He had become addicted to codeine. He had been receiving daily doses of the painkiller to relieve what must have been excruciating agony, and his body had become dependent on the opium derivative. He demanded more and more, even after his pain had abated somewhat. As Benzaquin tells it, his surgeon, Dr. Browder, took the cold turkey approach. Browder is reported as saying: "You're making yourself a bum. . . . You're not going to

---

*Paul Benzaquin, *Holocaust!* (New York: Holt, 1959).

be a bum on me. . . . I know when you've got pain . . . and I'll do something about it. But as of right this minute you're off the stuff in this hospital." According to Benzaquin, Clifford overcame his initial hostility to Dr. Browder and never again asked for codeine.

And he survived. During his stay at Boston City Hospital, he had six Red Cross nurses assigned exclusively to him, two per eight-hour shift, twenty-four hours a day. He had undergone more than one hundred transfusions. He was pumped up with countless quantities of saline solution and nutrients. At one point, his weight dropped to about 100 pounds from 165. The constant care had resulted in a medical miracle. He had battled with unimaginable pain, infection, shock, codeine addiction, depression, and suicidal impulses, and he had won.

After twenty-one months of treatment, skin grafts, and physical therapy, he was finally discharged, nearly as good as new. He had some physical souvenirs from the Grove—some scarring, a limp, and a small bald patch of burnt scalp. Clifford also had a new wife. He had met and fallen in love with a student nurse, Marion A. Donovan. They married and moved to his hometown of Sumner, Missouri.

Both hospitals were aware of the risk of shock, and both treated for it. But the doctors at Boston City Hospital stuck with the traditional approach to burn treatment. A few days after the fire, Dr. Charles Lund, chairman of Boston City's burns committee, issued a statement defending the conservative approach. He noted that ointments had been donated to the hospital unsolicited. But he added, "The surgeons of the Boston City Hospital appreciated the spirit behind these offers, but felt it unwise to use treatments with which they were not thoroughly familiar."

Unquestionably, Boston City Hospital was overburdened; it had to deal with 132 living patients, whereas Massachusetts General Hospital had only 39. Nevertheless, the difference in the mortality figures was striking. Just 7 of the 39 patients— about 18 percent—died at Mass General, all of them from respiratory complications. At Boston City, 39 of 96 patients—more than 40 percent—had died. Within months, Dr. Lund had become a convert. Surface treatment of the burns didn't matter as much as he had thought, he said. "I feel very strongly that the best surface treatment is one that does no harm and is comfortable for the patient," the doctor acknowledged. He added that he and his colleagues at Boston City had come to appreciate that such factors as sedatives, antibiotics, oxygen, fluid resuscitation, plasma transfusions, and humidity control were the most essential elements of effective initial treatment. Dr. Cope's daring experimental approach had prevailed.

It is a cliché to say that good things come out of terrible tragedies, but there was one very good result of the Grove fire: It led to giant strides in medical treatment. The disaster provided the medical community with a large-scale classroom in which to study of the effects of fire on human beings. Certainly, in modern practice, debridement is possible much sooner in the treatment process than Dr. Oliver Cope believed in 1942. Nevertheless, his courageous approach to treating the Grove's burn victims demonstrated to the medical community the necessity of treating the entire syndrome of bodily reactions—loss of fluids, edema, malnutrition, shock. In many ways, the knowledge gained by the Grove disaster is responsible for the fact that today victims with burns over 90 percent of their bodies have a good chance of survival.

However, there was more to be learned, and this time the new insight would come from Boston City Hospital.

All seven of the deaths at Mass General had resulted from respiratory complications. At Boston City, the thirty-nine deaths were attributed to a mix of severe burns *and* respiratory failure. Dr. Lund reported that very few had died from burns alone. During the first days after the fire, observers had been struck by the prevalence of what was described as a "pneumonia-like" condition that had afflicted many of the survivors.

This marked the beginning of the "poison gas" theory that has its adherents to this day. The origins of this "theory" might be traced to statements of Dr. Timothy Leary, the medical examiner for the southern Suffolk County district. Dr. Leary conducted ten autopsies of Grove victims and concluded that those who died immediately had succumbed to carbon monoxide poisoning. However, Leary speculated that those who had died more slowly might have been exposed to a lethal gas, similar to that used in chemical warfare. Dr. Lund of Boston City lent some additional credibility to this theory. "We don't know," he said, "whether the irritant was some specific gas, such as phosgene, which killed many soldiers in the last war, or was just a mixture of the products of combustion." It remained for one of Lund's colleagues at Boston City to develop "an alternative and simpler explanation."

Dr. Maxwell Finland interviewed seventy-two patients and painstakingly diagrammed their locations at the nightclub. His charts tended to refute the gas theory. The victims with lung damage were not in one localized area of the club but were distributed throughout the building, so there could be no single source of poison gas such as the cooling system's compressor. Moreover, the longer one was exposed to the fumes, the more severe the lung damage.

Finland thus arrived at his "simpler explanation." The dense, acrid smoke, containing hot gases and particles, and the length of the victims' exposure to it were the cause of the respiratory damage, not an exotic poison gas. "One need only consider" he wrote, "the effects of prolonged inhalation of very hot air and fumes which presumably contained many of the toxic products [from the burning wood, cloth, and plastic] . . . and, in addition, numerous hot particles of fine carbon or similar substances contained in the smoke." In effect, Finland had "discovered" the deadly effects of prolonged smoke inhalation, a phenomenon taken for granted now but which was not understood in 1942.

It is not quite accurate to say that there were only seven Grove deaths at Mass General, for there was the case of Francis Gatturna. Francis had suffered only superficial injuries, and he was promptly released from Mass General. However, his wife had been killed in the fire; she had died immediately, and her body had been brought to the Southern Mortuary. At first, Francis seemed reconciled to his loss, but by January 1 he was back at Mass General at his family's urging.

Drs. Stanley Cobb and Erich Lindemann, of Mass General's Department of Psychiatry, reported on Francis's behavior during his second hospital stay. They observed that he was racked by extreme tension, fear of death, violent urges, and guilt. Francis constantly recounted the events of that night to all who would listen. His wife had somehow fallen behind him while they were trying to escape. He had tried to help her, he repeated over and over again, but he had fainted, and the Grove crowd shoved him out.

In this respect, Francis was not unlike many other patrons, such as Ruth Strogoff, who saved themselves but lost their spouses. All such Grove patrons had to deal with the trauma of their personally terrifying experience as well as the grief of losing a loved one. Almost all of the patrons must have been struck by the sudden change from gaiety to stark terror, the seeming arbitrariness of who lived and who died, all compounded by the personal peril they felt.

However, unlike the others, Francis Gatturna was compelled to not only recall but actually relive in his mind this terrible event. Francis was unable to conjure up the fond memories of his wife, thoughts of the pleasurable times they had spent together, or perhaps recollections of some endearing idiosyncrasies—the kind of memories that soften the pain and reconcile the bereaved to their loss.

Instead, he was constantly inconsolable and muttered repeatedly, "I should have saved her or I should have died too." Nevertheless, his sessions with a psychiatrist seemed to yield results, suggesting that he would be able to cope. But Francis and his doctors needed more time, which unfortunately they would not have. "On the sixth day of his hospital stay," the psychiatric team reported, "after skillfully distracting the attention of his special nurse, he jumped through a closed window to a violent death."

As early as the post–Civil War period, physicians had noted in some soldiers a behavior that they quaintly labeled "nostalgia," a word that connotes a longing for a return to a pleasant place, or time, or experience. But for Francis and a number of others treated and studied by Cobb and Lindemann, there was no nostalgia but rather "intense subjective distress described as tension, loneliness or mental pain." These psychological disturbances were "precipitated by visits, by mentioning the deceased, and by receiving sympathy." The result in these patients was to "refuse visits lest they would precipitate the reaction, and to keep from one's thoughts all references to the deceased."

The Cobb-Lindemann study of the psychiatric observations of the Grove patients would be built upon in the years to come and provided the foundation for what is now called post-traumatic stress disorder. Harvard psychiatrist Alexandra Adler soon followed up the Cobb and Lindemann study with one of her own. She found that a year after the disaster, more than 50 percent of the survivors experienced "post traumatic neuroses" that were manifest in sleep disturbances, anxiety, survivor guilt, and generalized fears related to the fire.

It had all begun with Mass General's eighth Cocoanut Grove fatality, Francis Gatturna.

Another fatality of a Grove patron has a more tragic and ironic twist. Fourteen years after the fire, in 1956, Clifford Johnson, who had become a game warden in Sumner, Missouri, was driving home from work through the December snow. His vehicle skidded, ran off the road, overturned, and burst into flames.

This time, Clifford Johnson burned to death.

CHAPTER 11

Indictments—
General and Specific

"Happy New Year"

Mayor Maurice J. Tobin
to reporters following his grand jury appearance

JOHN O'FLANAGAN, the indictment clerk for the Superior Court of Suffolk County, spent much of the afternoon of December 31 shuttling back and forth between the grand jury room and the typing pool. This was the signal that indictments were imminent. The twenty-two grand jurymen had gone down to the wire. They had been selected on December 7, and their term ended this last day of the year, slightly more than one month after the fire. The failure of the jurors to return indictments by the end of the year would have required that the process begin anew the next year with a new panel.

Attorney General Bushnell and Suffolk County Assistant District Attorney Frederick T. Doyle had been presenting evidence jointly since the middle of the month. The state and county prosecutors culled many of their witnesses from the

Reilly hearings. All public officials who had testified before Reilly were called before the grand jury. Tobin and Reilly were themselves summoned. After his testimony, Tobin was asked what the grand jury had asked him. His only reply to the reporters was, "Happy New Year." Licensing board chair Mary E. Driscoll was also summoned before the grand jury. Miss Driscoll's testy reply to a reporter's question following her appearance was, "No, they didn't try to pin anything on me." (Mary Driscoll was a favorite of tavern owners because of her cooperative approach to regulatory matters. The son of one owner recalled years later that she was particularly fond of the extravagant hats that were her trademark. This tavern owner made it a point to give her one every Christmas, purchased from Boston's best millinery shop.)

Chief Justice John P. Higgins's courtroom was packed at 3:35 P.M., when the bills of indictment were formally presented. Then there was an unexpected delay. The courtroom fell silent as the judge pored over the presentments. He appeared troubled and confused by what he read. After conferring for some time with the prosecutors, Higgins finally turned to the grand jurors and said:

It is my understanding that you gentlemen have presented a statement. It is formally accepted as an honest expression of opinion of fellows who have given an important matter a great deal of time and thought. It is your expression of a subject which is of the utmost importance to the community. We appreciate the thought behind it and wish to express our appreciation for it. I wish you a Happy New Year.

The grand jury's "presentment" accompanying the specific indictments was a blanket denunciation of Boston's municipal officials. Bushnell's fingerprints were all but visible on this informal indictment. "We wish to record certain conclusions which the evidence compels us to draw," the grand jurors wrote. They said that they had "found no complete coordination between building department, fire department, police department, and licensing board with respect to the various types of inspection intended . . . to insure public safety." Instead, said the jurors, they had found "laxity and incompetence . . . [and that] officials in each department seemed to attempt to shift responsibility to some other department and visa versa." The jurors felt it necessary to make this statement "even though such evidence may fall short of establishing willfulness or corruption required to make neglect of duty a criminal offense." In other words, the jurors couldn't prove corruption, but they believed it existed.

During the following days, it would be rumored that there had been a push among the grand jurors to indict Maurice J. Tobin for bribery, but it had failed by a single vote. Since not much happens with grand juries that the prosecutors don't want to happen, Bushnell and Doyle had probably convinced the panel that, given the state of the evidence, indicting the mayor would be overreaching. The jurors would have to content themselves with scolding the city's officialdom.

As for the formal indictments, ten men were charged with crimes.

Barnett Welansky, James Welansky, and Jacob Goldfine, the Grove's wine steward, were indicted on twenty counts of involuntary manslaughter. Each count carried a sentence of up to twenty years. Barney's indictment was, of course, a foregone conclusion. As for Jimmy, the grand jury had not bought his explanation that he was only filling in for his brother. The jurors concluded that his "according to Hoyle" assurance that the New Broadway Lounge had been built in accordance with the approved plans and his negligent supervision of the overcrowded club on the night of the fire were sufficient to hold him responsible for the deaths.

The indictment of Goldfine for manslaughter was the big surprise. He was merely a salaried employee, his "wine steward" title a pretentious euphemism for bar manager. However, the grand jurors had concluded that Goldfine bore responsibility for the overcrowding and the locked doors on the night of the fire. He had been second in command under Jimmy on the night of the fire, and he had admitted that he had custody of all of the keys to the locked doors. In addition, he fit the description, given by an irate Grove patron, of the stocky, gray-suited man who had blocked the Grove's revolving door as the flames were licking up the staircase and had declared, "Nobody goes out until he pays his check."

Building Commissioner James H. Mooney was indicted for criminal neglect of his duty to enforce the building laws. Mooney, a disabled World War I veteran and president of the New England Building Officials Conference, had raised some eyebrows when he testified at the Reilly hearings. His department failed to supervise the Grove exits, he had said, because the nightclub did not charge admission. The building commissioner, who was not part of the Tobin-Reilly inner circle, was the highest-ranking city official indicted. The charge was a misdemeanor.

Building department inspector Theodore F. Eldracher was charged with two misdemeanors. The first indictment was for neglect of duty in failing to report insufficient exits. Eldracher, a city building inspector since 1922, apparently enjoyed hanging out at the Grove. He had previously admitted that he had visited the Grove on sixteen occasions between September 15 and November 25, and that he had known that the work "hadn't been completed" even though the new room had opened for business on November 17. He hadn't reported this, he said, because "it just slipped my mind." The second indictment was for conspiracy to violate the building laws.

The indictments of Mooney and Eldracher had probably insulated Mary Driscoll of the licensing board from criminal charges for licensing the New Broadway Lounge without the fusible fire doors and without an additional fire exit from the new room. Since these proposed changes required final approvals from the building department, her responsibility was obscured. As the grand jury said, "Officials in each department seemed to attempt to shift responsibility to some other department and visa versa."

Frank J. Linney, a fire department lieutenant since 1929, was charged with neglect of duty and accessory after the fact of manslaughter. Linney, the author of the notorious "condition—good" report, had made the implausible claim that he had tested the palm trees with a match eight days before the fire. He also had claimed to have carefully surveyed the club and decided that there were "sufficient" exits at the Grove. The accessory charge—the only other felony charge returned by the grand jury—stemmed from Linney's efforts to cover up his lax inspection.

Police Captain Joseph A. Buccigross was indicted for neglect of duty and failure to enforce fire laws, two misdemeanors. Buccigross, a police officer since 1919, had the misfortune of being on an "inspection tour" in civilian clothes on the night of the fire, when he might have taken steps to limit the size of the crowd. His boss, Police Commissioner Joseph F. Timilty, had tried to cover for Buccigross being in plain clothes by explaining that the captain was, in effect, under cover. "If he's looking for characters," said Timilty, "they would see him coming if he were in uniform."

Reuben O. Bodenhorn, the club's insouciant designer, was charged with conspiracy to violate the building laws in connection with construction of the New Broadway Lounge. Indicted along with Bodenhorn were two minor players: Samuel Rudnick, a contractor who had supervised the various Melody Lounge renovations and done the work on the New Broadway Lounge, and Rudnick's foreman, David Gilbert. Barney and Jimmy were also named in this indictment, but these misdemeanor charges were the least of their problems.

William Arthur Reilly, the fire commissioner for the City of Boston, had escaped the grand jury's inquiry unscathed. If Mayor Tobin had been indicted, his friend's fate might have been different. However, there was never any suggestion, as there had been with Tobin, that Reilly was on the take. Moreover, except for his temporizing on testimony like "Tobin and I fit" and other matters concerning the city's inner circle of politicians, Reilly's public investigation of the fire had been generally objective and professional. In addition, the indictment of his subordinate, Lieutenant Linney, put Reilly at a comfortable distance from responsibility.

As to which twenty people the Welanskys and Goldfine had killed, Bushnell and Doyle had the dubious luxury of choosing from 490 victims.*

The specific victims whom Barney, Jimmy, and Goldfine were accused of killing were carefully chosen for their locations, causes of death, and emotional impact. This enabled Bushnell and Doyle to underscore the lack of proper exits, the over-crowding, and the flammable materials in each area of the club. The prosecutors would mentally walk the trial jurors through the club so they could imagine—victim by victim—what it must have been like to have been a Grove patron on the night of November 28, 1942.

From the Melody Lounge: James Jenkins (burns) was last seen alive on the staircase from the Melody Lounge. Sydney E. McKenna (third-degree burns of the face and nose, and pulmonary complications) died three days after the fire. Hyman Strogoff (burns) died at the foot of the Melody Lounge staircase. These three victims would give the prosecutors the opportunity to focus on the overcrowding, the flammability of the satin ceiling, the inadequate exits, and of course, the locked fire door at the top of the staircase. They would be able to demonstrate how the inadequate exits in the Melody Lounge compounded the panic on the main floor.

From the foyer: Kathleen B. O'Neil (carbon monoxide poisoning, smoke inhalation) died behind the revolving door after losing her date's hand. Elisha Cobb (burns), a member of the

---

*As it would turn out, they would be tried for causing the deaths of nineteen people. The trial judge would drop the twentieth victim listed in the indictment—Madeline A. Wennerstrad—because no evidence was produced at trial about her death.

party of thirteen men who worked for General Electric who had just entered the Grove as the fire started, died behind the revolving door. The deaths in the foyer would emphasize the lethality of the revolving door and the fact that the side exit door was locked and concealed in the checkroom behind a coatrack.

From the main dining room: Mary H. Duggan (burns) was one of a party of twelve, seated on the Piedmont Street side of the dining room. Conrad Schorling (burns) and Mary Rose O'Sullivan (burns) decided to have one last dance moments before the fire overwhelmed the dining room. Joseph F. Swan (burns) was seated with his date at the near corner of the terrace. Ernest Bizzozero (carbon monoxide poisoning, smoke inhalation) was seated at the right side of the dining room with a party of fourteen celebrating the anniversaries of two couples. Alice Murray (burns), Josephine Donovan (burns), and Harold and Doris Ford (both burned) were all part of a party of fifteen people seated at the right-hand side of the dance floor near the stage; only one man from this group survived.

From the terrace: Anna Stern (respiratory burns) was part of the Buck Jones party. Adele Dreyfus (burns and smoke inhalation) and Eleanor Chiampa (burns and smoke inhalation) sat together on the terrace with Adele's husband and Eleanor's brother.

The deaths on the terrace and in the main dining room itself would give the prosecution the opportunity to offer evidence that the Venetian doors and extra tables and chairs blocked the Shawmut Street fire exit doors and that one of these doors was bolted shut.

From the New Broadway Lounge: Helen Griffen (carbon monoxide poisoning, smoke inhalation) was with her brother and two others who all got out safely. Pricilla White (pulmonary burns) had been sitting in the main dining room just at the passageway to the lounge; she followed her date into the lounge and was last seen alive in the center of the room. The new lounge was supposed to be protected by the fusible doors at the passageway and was required to have an exit to Shawmut Street. Barney had constructed a checkroom where this exit was supposed to have been. Pricilla White's body was found next to this checkroom.

In baroque legalese, the indictments charged, first, that the trio "on the twenty-eighth day of November in the year of our Lord Nineteen-Hundred-and-Forty-Two did, all and each of them, maintain, operate and supervise certain premises in the City of Boston, to wit: the Cocoanut Grove, so called." This allegation was an essential legal element required to prove manslaughter in this case. The trio—"all and each of them"—were in control of the premises, and therefore in control of decisions about decorations, doors, and room capacity. Each of the defendants had a defense against this charge. Jimmy would insist that he was filling in for his brother and knew nothing about alterations, wiring, decorations, or doors. Goldfine would argue that he was merely an employee, and an underpaid one at that. Barney, of course, wasn't there the night of the fire. Could his nearly two-week absence from the Grove get him off the hook?

The indictment went on to allege that the Grove was "an establishment for the sale of food and beverages" and that the three defendants "solicited and invited the patronage of [each of the twenty victims]." This allegation was intended to establish the defendants' legal duty of care that arose from their inviting the public onto the premises for business purposes. There would be no arguments on this issue.

The indictment closed with the following: "the said Barnett Welansky, James Welansky and Jacob Goldfine, all and each of them, did assault and beat the said [victim], and, by such assault and beating, did kill the said [victim] by willfully, wantonly, and recklessly maintaining, managing, operating and supervising the said premises." This last allegation was the heart of the indictment. Clearly, no one was arguing that Barney, Jimmy, or Goldfine had "assaulted and beat" anyone, at least in laymen's terms. And more importantly, no one was charging that any of the three defendants *intended* to kill—or even to "assault and beat"—anyone.

Intention to do harm is at the heart of criminal law. The crime of involuntary manslaughter, however, moves away from "intention" to the gray area of "recklessness." Mere "carelessness" is generally not a criminal matter; its redress is left to civil lawsuits. However, criminal law does punish actions that exceed carelessness but still fall short of fully developed "intention" to do harm. When a person's behavior is so insensitive to probable harmful consequences—in this case death—criminal liability attaches. The "willfulness" of the behavior is *not an intention to harm or kill* a person; it is *the intention to act recklessly*, heedless of the extraordinary danger the act creates.

Usually reckless conduct is an affirmative act, such as firing a gun without the intention to kill or harm but under circumstances where harmful consequences should be clearly foreseeable. But, as Bushnell would later tell the jury, "failure to act is as bad as acting." Barney, Jimmy, and Goldfine were indicted largely for things they had allegedly failed to do. These omissions could cost them, at a minimum, the next twenty years of their lives.

The trial date for the three defendants was set for March 15, 1943—a mere two and a half months after the indictments and less than four months after the fire.

There were both legal and practical reasons to try the case of *Commonwealth v. Barnett Welansky, James Welansky, and Jacob Goldfine* before the others.

The legal reason was that the other indictments were essentially derivative of the manslaughter charges. Unless the deaths were declared criminally unlawful, charges of violating or, in the case of the public officials, of not enforcing the building laws would be nearly impossible to prove.

The practical reason for prosecuting Barney, Jimmy, and Goldfine first was that, except for Linney's accessory charge, the charges against the other defendants were misdemeanors. Misdemeanor convictions would bring paltry punishments for the nearly five hundred deaths. A conviction in the manslaughter case—a species of criminal homicide under the law—was what the public wanted and what the tarnished political establishment needed.

CHAPTER 12

Recklessness

Of course, the government does not contend that the defendants intended to kill any of these victims. We are trying the involuntary type of manslaughter. They didn't intend to kill them, but they completely disregarded their rights.

Attorney General Robert T. Bushnell, opening statement

IN *THE STRANGER*, by Albert Camus, the novel's unsympathetic protagonist is accused of having murdered a man. At his trial, the focus shifts almost immediately from the circumstances of the murder to the "damning" evidence of the defendant's dastardly behavior and character—he had not demonstrated sorrow over his mother's recent death, and he had not cried at her funeral. This callousness, the prosecutor argues, proves that the accused is a threat to society and is therefore guilty of murder. He is found guilty and sentenced to death by beheading.

The irony of the novel lies in the fact that the defendant actually committed the murder. Nevertheless, the manner of his conviction is offensive to the reader because it ignores the defendant's acts and focuses instead on his "bad character." The specific intention to cause the alleged harm is at the heart of criminal law. In the Anglo-American system, the general rule is that a person may be convicted only by evidence showing he committed the acts that constitute the crime and that he intended the consequences of those acts. Evidence of a defendant's disposition or personality is generally considered prejudicial. In an early case, a Massachusetts judge explained that the reason for this rule is "to protect a party from the injustice of being called upon . . . to explain the acts of his life not shown to be connected with the offense with which he is charged."

However, that is only the general rule. To a certain extent, when "recklessness" is an element of a crime, the defendant's character becomes an issue.

There may be no more exasperating challenge for a criminal defense attorney than defending against a charge of "recklessness." Everything untoward a defendant has ever done—from peccadillo to cardinal sin and every misstep in between—can arguably be used to show that he was "heedless" of consequences. If Barney had been charged with premeditated murder—the ultimate crime of intention—evidence of his business history, his penchant for cost cutting and his micro-management style would have likely been ruled irrelevant. But recklessness is a slippery concept; it raises questions about the defendant's patterns of behavior, his choices, and ultimately, his overall character. Repeatedly, Bushnell and his team would argue with great success that every item of negative "evidence" about Barney's behavior tended to show a "reckless disregard" for the lives of his patrons.

The trial began on March 15, 1943. As they would every day for nearly the next four weeks, except Sundays and holidays, Barney and Jimmy Welansky and Jacob Goldfine sat in the defendants' dock behind their lawyers. Daniel J. Gallagher defended Jimmy, and Abraham C. Webber represented Goldfine.

Barney's counsel was his law partner, Herbert F. Callahan. The avuncular Callahan might have been one of Boston's best criminal defense attorneys, but this trial would test his mettle. He had a bad case and an unsympathetic client who had already been depicted in the press as a slippery character. Nevertheless, throughout the trial and Barney's subsequent ordeals, Callahan would prove himself not only a tenacious lawyer but also a loyal friend.

Things had gone badly for the defense even before the trial. Callahan had lost every preliminary skirmish between the New Year's Eve indictments and the start of the formal proceedings. He had filed a gale of papers challenging the indictment on technical legal grounds. He had argued that only the corporation that owned the Grove, not Barney, its controlling shareholder, could be held responsible; that Barney could not be indicted for an event that had occurred during his hospital stay; and that the commonwealth had failed to specify the connection between Barney's alleged recklessness and the deaths. All arguments in Callahan's bills of exception were met with indifferent judicial dismissals.

Attorney General Bushnell and Suffolk County Assistant District Attorney Frederick T. Doyle would prosecute the case on behalf of the Commonwealth of Massachusetts. Doyle, a journeyman prosecutor, would handle most of the trial, while Bushnell divided his time between strategic appearances in the courtroom and the grand jury investigation into the Boston police department's ties with Dr. Harry J. Sagansky, the dentist turned numbers racketeer. By the time the Grove trial started, Bushnell had already secured the indictment and arrest of Doc

Jasper. He would plead guilty later that week and receive a two-and-a-half- to three-year prison sentence. The former dentist had found the numbers racket much easier than pulling teeth. According to the 1955 report of a special crime commission of the Massachusetts Senate, Jasper had deposited $1,374,575.46 in one bank in 1942. Doc and his lieutenants paid fines totaling $31,475.

The attorney general was now focusing on the complicity of the city's police. Nevertheless, despite Bushnell's current preoccupation with the police scandal, he would always be at the Cocoanut Grove trial for the moments of high drama and maximum publicity.

Presumably because of the local political implications of the case, Judge Joseph L. Hurley was imported from distant Fall River to preside over the trial. Oddly, however, Hurley was a highly political type. He had served as the lieutenant governor under none other than James Michael Curley. However, the judge could not necessarily be considered a Curley partisan and, therefore, anti-Tobin. Curley had betrayed him during the 1936 state Democratic convention by reneging on his promise to support his lieutenant governor for the nomination to succeed him. Instead, Curley endorsed another man named Hurley.

For his part, Curley uncharacteristically passed on this excellent opportunity to bash Tobin and his administration. He was notably quiet about the Grove fire, which was understandable in light of Curley's lack of credibility on corruption issues. Curley was also restrained by the fact that, in the fluid world of Boston politics, many old Curley hands were part of the Boston political hierarchy. For instance, Police Commissioner Joseph F. Timilty had managed a number of his campaigns.

Judge Hurley presided over the selection of the twelve-man jury.* Fifty-two prospective jurors were interviewed. The judge asked how much they knew of the "so-called Cocoanut Grove disaster, which is common knowledge." Of course, all had heard of the fire. Most of those excused told the judge that they had formed an opinion as to the guilt or innocence—most likely the guilt—of the defendants. The judge ordered this decidedly working-class jury—among them a "repairman," a "shoe worker," a "mechanic," a "painter," and several "salesmen" (one of whom was chosen foreman)—to be sequestered at the Parker House for the duration of the trial.

The trial started badly for the defense. As soon as the jurors were excused at the end of the first day, Bushnell rose to ask Judge Hurley to permit them to visit the scene of the fire. Three days earlier, Barney had visited what was left of the Cocoanut Grove. The newspapers reported that he had been characteristically silent as he walked through the remains of the club, accompanied by the defense attorneys and an assistant attorney general. The defense lawyers no doubt decided then and there that the jury should not see these musty, debris-laden ruins.

Prosecutors revel in showing juries the gruesome details of an alleged crime. Defense attorneys, on the other hand, are usually prepared to stipulate that the crime occurred and to argue that photographs or visits to crime scenes are unnecessary and prejudicial to their clients.

---

*Women were not permitted to serve on Massachusetts juries until 1950. A bill to allow female jurors was introduced into the Massachusetts legislature for the first time in 1943. Bushnell endorsed the idea with characteristic rhetorical excess, declaring that it was "idiotic" to deny women the right to serve.

The lawyers for the three accused invoked the time-tested legal mantra of defense attorneys—that the resulting prejudice to the defendants outweighed the probative value of examining the premises. Callahan and the attorneys for Jimmy and Goldfine argued that the premises in no way resembled the condition of the Grove before 10:15 P.M. of that awful night. The lawyers asked how the defendants could get a fair trial after the jurors, their every step lit by portable lights, had climbed through the blackened wreckage of this once lively and gay nightspot. Goldfine's lawyer, Abraham C. Webber, predicted that the jury was "going to convict innocent men on what they see." Jimmy's lawyer, Daniel J. Gallagher, argued that the jury would become obsessed with the thought "that this is what the defendants have done." Gallagher even expressed concern for the jurors' safety.

Bushnell shrewdly retorted that this case was about the structure of the Grove, its layout and its doors, and added snidely that the defendants' true concern was to prevent the jury from examining the blocked and locked exits and seeing the areas where the never-constructed fire doors and an additional exit were supposed to have been. Judge Hurley granted the motion and expressed his confidence that the "intelligent men" on the jury could distinguish the effects of the fire-fighting efforts from the underlying conditions of the Grove.

The jury quietly visited the ruins the next morning. The group boarded a police bus at the courthouse for the short ride to Piedmont Street. Before they left, Bushnell had explained the layout of the club to the jurors, painstakingly pointing out each locked, blocked, or nonexistent exit. Judge Hurley, the three defense lawyers, and Assistant D.A. Doyle met the jurors at the Grove, where the judge instructed them to "stop, look, and listen." The group moved quickly through a driving rain to the protection of the marquee over the main entrance, the marquee topped with the now-scorched Cocoanut Grove sign.

The police had sealed and guarded the club since November 31, three days after the fire. However, the premises were not entirely sealed. The rolling roof had been opened during the fire and was still locked in that position. Other parts of the roof were pockmarked with the ventilation holes that had been poked by the firefighters. The months of rain and melting snow running into the ruins could only have intensified the grisly scene.

For the next several hours, these twelve "intelligent men" on the most sober of missions walked in the footsteps of the approximately 1,000 fun-seekers who had entered the Grove on November 28, 1942. How could they help but think, as attorney Gallagher had predicted, *This is what the defendants have done. Someone will have to pay.* Bushnell had won Round One.

The jurors were back in the courtroom for Bushnell's opening statement late that afternoon, their minds no doubt swirling with the images of the destruction that they had seen earlier. With a sheaf of notes in his hand and a plan of the Cocoanut Grove on an easel, the attorney general lived up to his formidable reputation, going on for two and a half hours, flaying the three defendants, particularly Barney, as he struck his themes:

Barney and the other two were in control of the premises on the night of the fire. Jimmy and Goldfine were present that night; they were in charge and could have controlled the number of people on the premises. Furthermore, Jimmy had dealt directly with the licensing board in connection with the New Broadway Lounge. "Up until 5PM on the day of the opening they had no liquor license at all," he told the jury. "The defendant

James appeared at the board just before closing time and assured the individual that everything was legal."

As for Barnett—never "Barney"—his hospitalization on the night of the fire and the twelve preceding days was of no legal consequence. Since 1933, Barnett C. Welansky had meticulously managed every aspect of the club. He was responsible for issuing standing orders that were followed on November 28. "There was nothing unusual that night," said Bushnell. Barney had ordered the doors locked and the exits obstructed "for more profit." Following long-standing practice, tables and chairs "were placed against doors, even on the dance floor as the hour of tragedy approached."

Bushnell then ticked off his formidable list of Barney's lies and omissions: He had failed to have flame-retardant chemicals applied to the fabrics. He had lied about the size of the crowds in license applications. He had expanded the Grove without permits and inspections. He had failed to install fire doors in the passageway to the New Broadway Lounge and had built a checkroom in the new lounge that obscured a fire exit. (The fusible fire doors to the New Broadway Lounge were a no-win dilemma for Barney. If the doors had been installed and then fused shut by the fire, the patrons in the new lounge would likely have been spared. But then all other patrons on the main dining room side would have been trapped in the corridor behind this door.)

Barney was disdainful of the law and the duties it imposed upon him, Bushnell told the jury. At this point, the attorney general alluded to the conversation with Harry Weene, who had told Barney that the electrical work in the New Broadway Lounge required a permit. Prudently avoiding the use of Mayor Tobin's name, Bushnell paraphrased Barney. "He said: 'It makes no difference. I fit with certain public officials. They owe me plenty.' This shows the state of mind of Barnett Welansky, how much he appreciated his duties to the public invited there nightly." There would be no railing in this trial about public corruption. Bushnell and the prosecution team would keep the spotlight on the acts of these defendants. This, of course, was a good legal tactic, but even as early as March 16, the focus on political responsibility for the tragedy was becoming blurred.

Also of no legal consequence was the fact that the Grove was technically owned and run by a corporation, said Bushnell. He would pierce the corporate veil. "That corporation, we'll show, was in truth and in fact only a legal fiction. It was an empty shell. We'll show Barnett Welansky actually controlled it all the time."

Of course, Bushnell missed no opportunity to appeal to emotions. His frequent provocative statements—for instance, patrons running around "like poor, trapped animals"—brought the three defense lawyers to their feet each time. Bushnell responded that he was "understating the situation if anything." These objections were sustained, but Bushnell continued to step over the line. At one point, the judge instructed the jurors that Bushnell's remarks were not evidence.

Anticipating the defense argument that the fire was not started by the three men in the dock, but by the sixteen-year-old bar boy, Bushnell said that the cause of the fire "was not material." Nor would he allow the defendants to use the ensuing panic as a defense, as they nevertheless would, much to Bushnell's obvious consternation. "Any reasonable person knows panics are to be anticipated in such cases. The exits were not exits. The whole thing constituted a trap. Lives were taken by the gross wanton and willful acts of the defendants in connection with that trap."

Bushnell went on with his tirade until 7 P.M. When the attorney general had concluded, Judge Hurley commended the jury on its stamina. By way of consolation, the judge reminded the jurors that the next day would be a day of rest since it was March 17, Evacuation Day, marking the expulsion of the British from Boston during the American Revolution, a legal holiday in Suffolk County that coincided with St. Patrick's Day.

When the trial resumed on March 18, the Bushnell-Doyle team began its neatly orchestrated presentation. To begin with, in case the jurors' memories of their visit to the Grove had faded, Doyle convinced the judge to admit 102 photographs taken after the fire. Despite the strong objections of the defense attorneys, Judge Hurley allowed the jury to examine the photos, with the vague admonishment that the pictures could be considered only to demonstrate the "effect of the burning."

The prosecution then moved on to its "corporation-as-empty-shell" theory. Katherine Welch and Jennie Welansky, the two "dummy" directors, were called to testify that they had no idea about the operations of the New Cocoanut Grove Inc., had never attended meetings, and didn't even hold the stock that had been issued in their names. Jennie admitted under questioning that "Barnett took care of matters."

Then Mary Driscoll of the licensing board was called to the stand. Her memory was foggy, she said. She admitted, in a roundabout manner, that she had signed the license extension for the New Broadway Lounge at about five o'clock of its opening day. "I have the statement of a competent clerk," she said, "but I cannot say, under oath, that I remember it." Nor could she quite recall seeing the newspaper advertisement that morning announcing the opening and then ordering her clerk to call the Grove to remind Jimmy that the license hadn't been formally issued. On cross-examination, Callahan asked Miss Driscoll the very salient question about what steps she had taken to assure that the plans had been complied with before granting the license. The judge did not permit her to answer.

Although they were generally sympathetic to Barney, several Grove employees damaged his case. The main-floor waiters' captain, Leo S. Giovanetti, testified that six extra tables were put on the dance floor and that five additional waiters had been hired for the evening. He said the tables blocking the Venetian doors were the "usual setup." The New Broadway Lounge waiters' captain, Salvatore Accursio, told how fifty to seventy-five people had to be turned away from that room, some because they were underage but many because the new lounge was packed. A handyman told of Barney's standing instructions to lock the service door by 7 P.M. each evening. Anne Lentini, the foyer checkroom girl, identified the coatrack that was placed across the exit door every night. She explained how it had blocked her escape and how she had run through the revolving door with her hair aflame. She also mentioned in passing that Jacob Goldfine's nightly practice was to collect the money in her tip can, a statement the judge allowed as an indication of Goldfine's control over employees, but which must have told the jurors something about his character.

Firemen and patrons testified about the fire and its effects, creating, as might be expected, vivid images of the panic and awful deaths. Lest the jurors forget the human toll, the prosecutors brought to the stand witnesses, many dressed in mourning black, who told of the last minutes before they lost their husbands, wives, or friends.

The one light moment came with the testimony of Navy Ensign Bill T. Connery of Dubuque, Iowa. Connery had been standing at the Melody Lounge bar talking with some girls. When the fire erupted, he ran through the kitchen and into the refrigerator. "I met Lieutenant John Carr and his wife there. They were from Iowa too," said Bill in his wide-eyed, Midwestern manner.

Then there was the testimony that the *Boston Herald* described as "so gruesome, the court heard it only out of necessity." The Suffolk County medical examiners blandly recited the causes of death of the nineteen victims: asphyxiation . . . carbon monoxide poisoning . . . cooked inside and out . . . burns of the face, neck, breasts, arms, and legs . . . burns of the larynx, trachea, and bronchi . . . edema.

Henry Weene, the neon lighting specialist, retold his story that Barney had said that no permit was required for the New Broadway Lounge because "Tobin and I fit." This time, however, Weene added that Barney had also said, "They owe me plenty." Callahan jumped on this new information. During cross-examination, Callahan asked why Weene hadn't mentioned that Barney had said, "They owe me plenty" at the Reilly hearings. "I didn't get a chance to," said Weene. "There was so much commotion in the hearing room." Callahan and Gallagher took turns going after him pitilessly, but Weene stuck to his story. Gallagher closed his cross-examination, his face nearly touching Weene's, by saying, "The fact of the matter is that Barnett Welansky never made any such statement about Mayor Tobin. He never said such a thing. That's the God's honest truth, isn't it?" Weene didn't skip a beat. "No, it's not the truth," he fired back.

An architect was called to testify that Barney had not followed the plans approved by the building department for the New Broadway Lounge and that he obviously had no intention to do so. Welansky had installed seats in the precise spot where the fusible doors were supposed to have been. Moreover, he had built a checkroom that hid and blocked an exit to Shawmut Street. Once again, the question of the building department's nonfeasance hung in the air.

Then Stanley Tomaszewski took the stand. Stanley's testimony might provide Callahan with a line of defense he had attempted unsuccessfully to pursue until now. He would pin the fire on Stanley. Following the gentle questioning by Assistant District Attorney Doyle, where the boy calmly recited his now-familiar story, Callahan began his cross-examination. "There is no doubt," he said to Stanley, "but that you lighted a match which started the fire." Doyle objected and Judge Hurley ruled the "question" out of order. Callahan tried repeatedly to nail the boy, but Stanley was by this time an experienced witness. He couldn't be sure what caused the fire, he said repeatedly in response to Callahan's hostile questions. The judge ruled out of order every effort by Callahan to question Stanley about what Callahan claimed were the boy's "prior inconsistent statements."

No issue illustrates Callahan's problem of distinguishing between Barney's character flaws and his specific guilt more clearly than his frustrating skirmishes over testimony about the Grove's electrical wiring.

Bernard B. Whelan, superintendent of the fire department's Wire Division, may have been the sole Boston civil servant ever to do his job as it related to the Cocoanut Grove. On November 7, three weeks before the fire, Whelan had sent a letter to the Grove stating that "persons unfamiliar to this Division" were doing the electrical work in the New Broadway Lounge without a permit. Another warning letter was sent on November 17, the day the New Broadway Lounge opened. A final "cease and desist" order was scheduled to be served on November 30, two days after the fire. The order would have affected only the New

Broadway Lounge. Even though no evidence would ever be presented that the unauthorized work in the new lounge had any connection to the fire—it was universally acknowledged that the fire had begun in the Melody Lounge—Whelan was permitted to testify over Callahan's strenuous objections.

To make matters worse, electrical expert H. C. Witherell, director of the state board of examiners for electricians, gave even more damaging testimony. Witherell painted a graphic picture of the makeshift shoddiness behind the Grove's romantic façades. He testified that some electrical equipment was ungrounded, that 60-amp fuses were used in 15-amp circuits, that lamp cord was used where armored cable should have been, and that junction boxes were hidden in false ceilings. "It is hard to understand why they hadn't had a fire before," Witherell testified, leaving the implication that the sloppy wiring had caused the fire.

Callahan, understandably, became nearly apoplectic over this testimony, and for good legal reasons. There had been some undocumented reports that a wall near the palm tree in the Melody Lounge had been unusually hot, perhaps from defective wiring, well before Stanley had approached with his match. But testimony about the heated wall never made its way into the trial. The prosecutors, therefore, never met their legal burden of demonstrating "proximate cause"—a plausible connection between the substandard wiring and the fire. Although Callahan did succeed in getting Whelan and Witherell to admit that they had discovered no connection between the electrical wiring and the fire, the damage was done: The jurors were free to conclude that this evidence showed that Barney was sloppy, heedless of consequences.

CHAPTER 13

Ex Post Facto

It is very easy, after a thing happens, to be wise about it.

Defense attorney Herbert F. Callahan

ON APRIL 2, it was Callahan's turn. The commonwealth had rested its case the day before. In a little more than two weeks, the prosecution had paraded ninety-four witnesses before the jury.

The quietly blood-chilling description of Frederick W. Harrington was typical of the survivors' testimony, underscoring as it did the hopelessness that so many had faced. He had been with a party of fifteen people in the main dining room, celebrating the wedding anniversaries of two couples. Harrington was the only member of the party who was standing at the moment the fire crossed the ceiling from the Caricature Bar, and that small difference had saved him. "I yelled to my party to follow me," he said. "Did they?" he was asked. "No," he replied softly. He was the sole survivor of the group, which included five siblings and their spouses. As far as Harrington knew, all of his companions had died in their seats, apparently too stunned to react in the seconds before they burned to death. Testimony like this had made vivid Bushnell's depiction of the victims dying "like poor, trapped animals."

Virtually all employees and patrons who testified had been asked to estimate the number of people in the club that night. Estimates varied, but all were too high for the defense: Melody Lounge, 250 to 400 people, three to five and six deep around the bar; the main dining room, 400 to 500 people; the New Broadway Lounge, up to 250 people. (In addition, there were at least 80 employees on duty that night.) The defense lawyers objected that these laypersons had no expertise in crowd estimation, but to no avail.

In addition, the prosecution had brought parts of the Cocoanut Grove to court, piece by piece—the scorched Venetian doors, fragments of electrical wiring, the burnt Melody Lounge palm tree, the Piedmont Street exit door with the tongue lock, and the revolving door. Each piece of this demonstrative evidence had been supported by damning testimony. Fireman William A. Hughes, for instance, told the grisly story of pulling twelve to fifteen bodies from the Melody Lounge staircase after the tongue lock had been smashed open.

Barney was being buried under the weight of the evidence.

On one occasion, Callahan himself was put on the defensive. On the question of the Grove's wandering record books, Rose Gnecco (Ponzi), the Grove's bookkeeper, testified that she had taken the books from the police station and brought them to Callahan's office in cartons tied with rope. She had done this, she said, at the instruction of the Boston police brass. Referring to the tied boxes, Callahan asked her, "Were they ever opened?" Mrs. Gnecco replied that she didn't know. However, she added that she had examined the books at state police headquarters after they had been in Callahan's possession. She had found that the book listing the Grove's charge accounts was missing. Callahan moved on to other subjects.

Frustrated at nearly every effort to soften the harsh picture that had been drawn of Welansky, Callahan had only one line of defense left. He would blame everyone else—public officials, materials suppliers, employees, and finally, the victims themselves.

First, he would try to pin responsibility on a civil servant. Callahan called to the stand a trembling Lieutenant Frank Linney, who was himself under indictment for his November 20 "condition—good" report and for his alleged subsequent cover-up. On the opening day of the trial, Linney had been seated in the defendants' dock with the Welansky brothers and Goldfine. However, his attorney had argued successfully, and with Bushnell's acquiescence, that Linney's case should be severed—he could hardly be an accessory after the fact of manslaughter unless manslaughter had been proved first.

Now, a shaking Linney took the stand as a subpoenaed witness. He answered the first three questions put to him in a barely audible voice—his name, address, and occupation. Then he responded to all of Callahan's other questions, slowly and deliberately so as not to stumble, "I refuse to answer on the advice of counsel on the ground that it might tend to incriminate me."

Callahan and his co-counsels argued to the judge that Linney had waived his Fifth Amendment rights by having testified publicly before the Reilly inquest, but Judge Hurley upheld Linney's right to invoke his right against self-incrimination.

Callahan had hoped to use Linney as a shield for Barney. Had Linney testified about his "inspection," Callahan could have credibly argued that public officials like Linney, who after all knew more about fires and building structures, had not warned Welansky of the dangerous conditions at the Grove. In fact, Linney had reported that conditions were "good." Instead, Callahan had succeeded only in showing Linney—an alleged co-conspirator—as too frightened to testify and implicitly admitting his guilt.

To make matters worse, the judge ruled that there was no proof that Barney knew about or relied on Linney's report of his "inspection" eight days before the fire; he declined to allow the report into evidence.

A frustrated Callahan then pressed his argument that it was panic, not Barney's actions, that had caused the deaths. Bernard Levin's wife and four other companions had died at the Grove. Coincidentally, Levin had been at the Grove on its opening night in 1927. "I was at the opening and at the closing," he noted sadly. Levin testified about the panic that had gripped the crowd: "The people seemed to have utter disregard for everything and everybody. I cried, 'For God's sake, take it easy or we'll all get killed.'"

Other friends and relatives of the victims were called by Callahan to testify similarly about the terror and chaos. Bushnell and his team wisely passed on cross-examining Levin and the others who had been patrons at the Grove, and who had suffered personal losses. But this was not the case with Herbert Schwartz.

Schwartz had been a passerby who helped pull victims out of the New Broadway Lounge. He testified that he had seen a woman who was trying to escape the flames repeatedly being pulled back into the Grove by other terrified patrons. He recited this story and told about the assistance he had rendered at the Grove for nearly five hours.

Schwartz was a good citizen. He was also a well-prepared defense witness. Nearly every sentence he uttered under Callahan's guidance had invoked images of panic: "The crowd was mad. There was no controlling them whatsoever. . . . They were jumping on top of one another and it was impossible to help them. . . . It was just wild panic."

Through this series of witnesses, culminating with Schwartz, Callahan hoped to develop a theme first introduced by Building Commissioner Mooney at the Reilly inquest only days after the fire. Mooney, since indicted for neglect of duty, had testified that it was his opinion that there were sufficient exits at the Grove, enough for 1,300 people in fact. Panic had prevented most of the victims from reaching those exits, Mooney had said.

Would the jury buy this defense? Bushnell was taking no chances. After delivering his stem-winding opening statement three weeks earlier, Bushnell had taken a back seat for most of the trial, allowing Frederick T. Doyle to methodically build the commonwealth's case. Now, with his work at the grand jury investigating the links between Doc Jasper and the Boston police finished, he would jump back in with both feet.

Planting himself directly in front of Schwartz, he began his cross-examination. The witness's credibility began to slip with the first question. Schwartz acknowledged that his father owned a tavern just down the street from the Cocoanut Grove, suggesting a personal connection with Barney.

Then Bushnell carved up this defense witness piece by piece:

"Do you know the Welanskys?"

"Yes," Schwartz answered.

"How long have you known them?"

"I've known Barney for about 10 years."

"To whom did you first tell this story?"

"Mr. Gallagher [Jimmy's attorney], I believe," Schwartz told him.

"You didn't volunteer it to the Boston fire department hearing or to any of the other investigators."

"No."

"How did you happen to tell Mr. Gallagher?"

"I happened to drop into an office, and he was there."

"You wanted to help the Welanskys?" ventured Bushnell.

"Not necessarily," Schwartz countered.

"What office was this?"

"It was Mr. Welansky's office [it was also Callahan's office], and Mr. Gallagher was there."

"You just told your story and then you got a summons, is that it?"

"That's it," Schwartz concluded.

Now Bushnell's voice rose to a roar that was heard in the corridors outside of the courtroom: "Has anyone told you to repeat the word panic, panic, panic?" Schwartz replied in quiet protest, "Nothing of the sort."

By extracting the admissions from Schwartz that he was a part of the small circle of Boston bar and nightclub owners that included Barney, and that he had "happened to drop into" the Welansky-Callahan office to volunteer his testimony, Bushnell had rendered irrelevant the witness's "observations" about the panicked crowd.

Joseph Dobesch, the materials supplier and installer, took the stand to testify that the orange velour material that he had provided to line the walls of the passageway to the New Broadway

Lounge was flame retardant. Dobesch brought with him a 3-by-3-foot sample of the material. Callahan's examination went well:

Callahan: "The sample that you brought here was from a roll of material that was used at the Cocoanut Grove?"

"Yes," Dobesch offered.

"And it was purchased by you as flameproof?"

"Yes."

"And it was installed by you in the Cocoanut Grove as having been flameproofed, is that correct?" Callahan continued.

"Yes," the witness replied without hesitation.

Callahan asked the witness to demonstrate that the fabric was "flameproof." Dobesch touched a lit match to the folded fabric. It smoldered and went out.

With three leading questions and this small demonstration, Callahan had placed Dobesch between Barney and responsibility for at least a part of the fire. But it would be a short-lived victory.

When it came to Bushnell's turn, he performed the same "test," but this time he unfolded the material. It immediately burst into flame and emitted black smoke that filled the courtroom. Bushnell could only hold onto the sample long enough to ask Dobesch, "Did you say this material had been treated with flame retardant?"

Dobesch answered, "Yes."

"Then when is it going to start to retard?" demanded Bushnell. The courtroom erupted in laughter, and so did the witness, who did not answer.

With tears running down his face, Bushnell milked the moment for all it was worth. "This is too hot for me," he yelled. Then he dropped the burning fabric to the floor and asked,

"Will it explode?" "No," Dobesch replied sheepishly. Bushnell then began to stamp on the burning remnant. Jimmy's lawyer, Daniel Gallagher, sprang up and shouted, "Don't kick that! That's an exhibit!" Judge Hurley made his unsolicited ruling: "He'll stamp it out. We can't have a fire in the courtroom." Jurors and spectators were coughing, and the judge ordered a recess so that court officers could open every window to clear the smoke.

Herbert F. Callahan had probably decided very early, perhaps even before the trial had begun, that Barney would have to take the stand in his own defense. For a criminal defense attorney, there is no more painful decision than to advise a client to waive his Fifth Amendment right not to testify. However, Callahan must have known that, barring a miracle, he would have no other choice.

He had performed no miracles. Far from it. Linney's assertion of his Fifth Amendment rights, Schwartz's lack of credibility, and Dobesch's smoldering fabric had been serious setbacks. Dobesch's testimony had quite literally failed the laugh test.

On the morning of April 7, Callahan called for Barnett C. Welansky to take the witness stand. Observers noted that the usually rumpled Barney was particularly well groomed that day. The defense attorney led Barney through a systematic denial of all of the damaging evidence against him.

Barney related how he had been hospitalized since before the opening of the New Broadway Lounge and that he was nowhere near the Grove on the night of the fire. He wept at his first reference to his illness. He said he had never told Harry Weene, the neon light man, that he didn't have to follow the rules because "Tobin and I fit. They owe me plenty." That was a lie, he protested.

He had shown the letter from the Wire Division about the electrical work in the new lounge requiring a permit to his contractor, Samuel Rudnick. He said Rudnick had assured him that "We'll take care of it."

Similarly, Barney claimed that he didn't know about the lack of permits for the various renovations of the Melody Lounge over the years. He left those things up to Rudnick, who was himself under indictment for conspiracy to violate the building laws. As for the flammable materials, "Mr. Bodenhorn said everything was flameproof." Barney testified that Goldfine was a $40-a-week employee and Jimmy was at the Grove out of fraternal loyalty and against Barney's wishes. "I asked James not to go there at all," said Barney.

He was a law-abiding businessman, he said, and over the years the premises had been inspected by numerous state and city inspectors without adverse report. And Barney claimed that Frank Balzarini, his headwaiter who had died in the fire, had been instructed to see that the emergency exit doors were unlocked.

Under nearly five hours of friendly direct examination, Barney had given a good account of himself. However, now he had to face Robert T. Bushnell.

"The headwaiter, now deceased":

BUSHNELL: Did you give any instruction to anybody to keep [the Melody Lounge] door unlocked?

BARNEY: Yes, the headwaiter [Frank Balzarini].

BUSHNELL: He's dead?

BARNEY: I understand so.

BUSHNELL: It's a fact, isn't it?

BARNEY: Yes.

BUSHNELL: You instructed the headwaiter, now deceased, to come out of the main dining room and leave his other duties and make sure the door leading out from the Melody Lounge was kept unlocked.

BARNEY: Yes.

BUSHNELL: Did he have charge of any other [doors]?

BARNEY: He had general charge of all doors.

BUSHNELL: That included downstairs?

BARNEY: No, I suppose the chef had charge of the door in the kitchen.

BUSHNELL: At least the headwaiter, now deceased, had no responsibility for the door leading into the alleyway [the door blocked by the sewer pipe that bartender John Bradley said "nobody thought about"].

BARNEY: No.

BUSHNELL: Anyone have?

BARNEY: One of the bartenders was supposed to see if it was locked before he left for the night.

BUSHNELL: Which bartender was that?

BARNEY: Oh, Charlie Mitchell.

BUSHNELL: Did you instruct Mitchell to have anything to do with the door?

BARNEY: In a general way.

BUSHNELL: He's dead.

BARNEY: Yes, he died.

The locked door at the head of the Melody Lounge stairway:

BUSHNELL: When you had that door put in, did you contemplate it should be used as an exit for the Melody Lounge?

BARNEY: I did.

BUSHNELL: Why equip it with a tongue lock and a panic lock?

BARNEY: I didn't know it at the time.

BUSHNELL: You have opened that door yourself?

BARNEY: Yes.

BUSHNELL: You heard later that the firemen had to break it down, didn't you?

BARNEY: I read it in the newspapers.

BUSHNELL: Did you find out who did it [locked the door]?

BARNEY: I can't explain it.

The Grove's seating capacity:

BUSHNELL: In these applications you filed with the licensing board did you state what you considered to be the accurate seating capacity?

BARNEY: I don't know.

BUSHNELL: Now in this application here you stated there were 100 tables.

BARNEY: In the main dining room.

BUSHNELL: You meant the main dining room and not the entire licensed premises on which you were applying to do business?

BARNEY: Well, the dining room mainly.

BUSHNELL: You didn't intend to include other parts and rooms of the club?

BARNEY: I don't know.

BUSHNELL: Are there more than 100 tables in those two rooms?

BARNEY: It seems that there were more than that.

BUSHNELL: Now, on the 400 chairs given, that's not correct either.

BARNEY: No, I think it seemed there were more than that.

BUSHNELL: Now, continuing, you are asked in this application to state the number of fixed stools and you gave 30, is that right?

BARNEY: Yes.

BUSHNELL: How many in the Caricature Bar?

BARNEY: 80, I guess.

BUSHNELL: Why, you made no effort at all to answer the questions correctly, did you?

BARNEY: I didn't think it was material, no.

BUSHNELL: Read the statement at the end of this application.

BARNEY: "I warrant the truth of the foregoing statements under penalty of perjury."

BUSHNELL: Did you write the answers on this form?

BARNEY: Yes.

The effect of Barney's hospitalization on the night of the fire:

BUSHNELL: You weren't worried about the Cocoanut Grove [while in the hospital], is that it?

BARNEY: No, Frank Balzarini, Rose Gnecco, and Jack [Goldfine] knew their duties, and things would go on whether I was there or not.

BUSHNELL: In other words, you felt you had set the machinery in motion and it would go on whether you were there or not?

BARNEY: Yes.

Barney's "inheriting" the Grove:

BUSHNELL: Did you buy the stock in the corporation then [after King Solomon's death]?

BARNEY: It was given to me.

BUSHNELL: Who gave it to you?

BARNEY: His wife. The estate didn't want it, and I spoke with [Norfolk Probate Court] Judge McCoole about it, and I got a bill of sale of all of their interests in the Cocoanut Grove.

BUSHNELL: Any petition ever filed, or any record on which the judge passed?

BARNEY: No.

BUSHNELL: You know Judge McCoole's also deceased.

BARNEY: Yes.

At first, Barney had fought back as Bushnell blazed away with questions that carried to every corner of the courtroom. Near the end, he didn't answer some questions at all. At times, he mumbled in a voice too low for the jurors to hear, and Judge Hurley told him to speak up.

After nearly a day and a half of direct and cross-examination, Barney was back in the defendant's dock. The defense rested. The three attorneys for the defense made their motions for directed verdicts of not guilty. After they had made their arguments, Bushnell stood up and said only, "I do not wish to be heard." Judge Hurley promptly denied the motions. All that was left were summations, the judge's charge to the jury, the jury's deliberations—and the verdicts.

As he prepared his summation for the next day, Herbert Francis Callahan knew what he would tell the jury. He would tell them what all defense attorneys tell jurors. He would say that he was confident that they would acquit his client. He would explain to them that they had no other reasonable choice. But Callahan must have known that he would have to call upon every ounce of optimism within him to believe that.

An already-bad case had further deteriorated with Barney's testimony.

Barney had filled the holes in the prosecution's case. Welansky had admitted that the management system that he had set in motion before the fire assured in his mind that "things would go on whether I was there or not." This had undermined the contention that his absence from the Grove for twelve days before the fire absolved him of responsibility. His answers that the exits were the job of the brave Frank Balzarini—"the headwaiter, now deceased"—and his admitting to filing false seating data had further weighed him down. His defense for the flammable materials and the lack of permits—that those were Bodenhorn's and Rudnick's jobs—sounded like passing the buck at the very least. Yet, as damaging as his testimony had been, Barney's denials and evasions were the only "evidence" that Callahan could hang his hat on.

On the morning of April 9, Callahan rose to begin a summation that would last more than three hours. Through forceful language, and by taking liberties with the evidence, he took his best shot.

He opened by acknowledging "that on the night of November 28, 1942, there occurred the most horrible catastrophe that has ever happened in these parts." He then reminded the jury that Bushnell had himself said that the charge was not of intentional killing but of recklessness. The question, Callahan offered, was whether this "horrible catastrophe" could have been reasonably foreseen.

"It is very easy, after a thing happens, to be wise about it," he said, expressing the difficulty of defending against a charge of recklessness. "No man could have reasonably anticipated that what happened at the Cocoanut Grove on the night of November 28 would have happened and should be guarded against," he told the jury.

The public servants hadn't foreseen the danger, he said. "Here's a man conducting a business that's open for inspection practically every hour of every day. If there had been anything wrong, you would think that some of the authorities who take care of those things would have disclosed it."

As for Weene's charge that Barney had said, "Tobin and I fit. They owe me plenty," Callahan told the jury that Weene had lied. "Welansky said he didn't say that—that it was a lie." Weene had told his story several times, he said, and each time it had been slightly different. "Well, if he did fit with Mayor Tobin," Callahan suggested, "he didn't fit very long, because the job hadn't been going on very long before a notice came in from the wire department telling him he needed a permit."

Callahan took some liberties with the evidence about locked doors. Ignoring the testimony that there were at least twelve dead bodies on the staircase, he said, "There is no evidence that anyone tried to use the Melody Lounge door. There is no evidence that Welansky ever ordered that door to be locked. The evidence is that as far as he knew, that door was open. He didn't want it locked with a tongue lock."

Barney had relied on the expertise of others, and they had let him down: "Can it be said that he should have anticipated a conflagration which started a stampede? No one had told us yet how that fire traveled so fast. Welansky had been told [by Bodenhorn] the material was flameproof. If it was not, it was no legal fault of his. Welansky used reasonable care in conducting those premises." As for the lack of permits for the New Lounge renovations, Barney had "called in his friend, Mr. Rudnick," said Callahan. "He did what you and I would do. He told him what he wanted and said, 'Go ahead and do it.'"

The loss of life was caused by panic, he said. "A patron turned off a bulb, and a boy, Stanley, lighted a match. Then what happened? Panic! People running to get out. You heard a witness say 'It was every man for himself.' People were acting like wild animals. People were knocked down and trampled on. Many who did use their heads did get out. It was an occasion of terror, and once terror prevails, there is no telling what can happen. . . . People were killed by crowds that night."

Assistant District Attorney Frederick T. Doyle had let Callahan go on for several hours without objecting to his dubious interpretations of the "evidence." When it came his turn, Doyle, an enormous bear of a man, paced back and forth along the jury box for a mere eighty minutes, punctuating each of his points by a slam of his hand on the rail.

Just as Callahan had done, Doyle opened with a reminder to the jury that it was sitting in judgment of a landmark case. "November 28 will go down in history as a date to be remembered throughout the land," he said.

This was no accident, said Doyle, and it was "ludicrous" to say so. Then, with a dramatic wave of his arm toward the defendants, he said, "The place was a firetrap, and the people responsible for it sit in that dock."

"Barnett Welansky was in charge there since 1933," said Doyle. "He rigged the entire proposition. He set it up."

Doyle described the 6,000 square feet of fabric throughout the Grove and then took advantage of one of Barney's verbal gaffes. Bushnell had asked Barney about the flame resistance of that material. Barney's awkward response had sounded callous. "This was no concern of mine," he had said, meaning that he had relied on the advice of his suppliers. Doyle capitalized on this slip and asked the jurors rhetorically whether they doubted "that the place was stocked chockablock full of inflammable material? Well it burned, didn't it? . . . Do you want any better explanation than that? And it went up like a forest fire. Couldn't you stop right there and say, 'These people did invite people for pay into their place of business, and *it was no concern of theirs* whether it was flame-resistant or treated or not?'"

The locked and obstructed doors had sent the victims to an early grave, he said. The ad that had announced the opening of the "breathtaking" new lounge should have read, "Come to the Cocoanut Grove and be packed in like sardines . . . come where the doors are locked." The doors were kept locked "for profit," to "keep some kid from running out without paying the check." Among the decorations, there was only one thing missing, he offered. "Accompanying a skull and cross bones over the Melody Lounge door should have been the sign which Dante inscribed over the Gates of Hell—Abandon hope all ye who enter here."

Referring to Barney's contention that Frank Balzarini had been charged with seeing that the doors were not locked, Doyle told the jurors, "Do you think that if it was the headwaiter's duty to keep the door open it would have been locked that night? . . . Why, he died when he went back there again and again that night. They can't defile his memory."

Doyle was most animated about the panic defense. He reminded the jurors that Callahan had said in his summation that those "who kept their heads" survived. He shot back sarcastically, "Well, Goldfine and James Welansky got out."

The panic argument was, he said, "a libel on the dead."

"And all day you have been filled up with smooth talk about panic. What did they expect people to do? Stand up and be burned to death? They ran to one door. It was locked. They ran to another. It was locked. . . . Instead of a place of entertainment you'd think it was hermetically sealed to keep people in."

The defendants, particularly Barney, were motivated by greed, said Doyle. "They were not satisfied with $1,000 a night. . . . There wasn't a penny to be lost—utilizing every bit of space for tables, overcrowding there, and then taking and blocking up an exit door [with the coatrack] for a dime a head . . . or $3.20 for the night."

CHAPTER 14

The Verdict

Even if a particular defendant is so stupid or so heedless
. . . that in fact he did not realize the grave danger, he cannot escape the imputation of wanton or reckless conduct.

Judge Joseph L. Hurley's jury instruction

ON APRIL 10, all preliminaries had ended, and it was at last
time for Judge Hurley to deliver his instructions to the
jury. He started by reminding the jurors—dubiously—that "this
is not an attempt to find someone on whom to pin the blame. It
is not an attempt to find a scapegoat for public vengeance." The
judge then moved on to define the elements of the crime of involuntary manslaughter in language that henceforth would be
read by virtually every law student.

First, there was the subjective definition of the crime, the defendant's knowledge of the risk, and his conscious decision to
ignore it:

To constitute wanton or reckless conduct . . . grave danger to
others must have been apparent, and the defendant must have

chosen to run the risk . . . no matter whether the ordinary man would have realized the gravity of the danger or not.

Under this definition of the crime, the jury might conclude that Barney *knew* that the locked and blocked exits, the uninstalled fusible doors, and overcrowding presented a "grave danger" to the patrons. They might find that he nevertheless chose to run the risk and was therefore guilty, no matter what an "ordinary man" would have done.

However, the judge pointed out that there was also an objective, ex post facto element, reflected in Callahan's lament, "It is very easy, after a thing happens, to be wise about it." Here the court was invoking the law's notion of the "reasonable man" test. Under the common law, this hypothetical person is the average person who is informed about the demands of society, aware of its legal requirements, and fair-minded.

> But even if a particular defendant is so stupid or so heedless . . . that in fact he did not realize the grave danger, he cannot escape the imputation of wanton or reckless conduct . . . if an ordinary man under the same circumstances would have realized the gravity of the danger. A man may be reckless within the meaning of the law although he himself thought he was careful.

In other words, ignorance was no excuse. The jurors were instructed to ask, what would the hypothetical "ordinary man" have done in Barney's situation? Could Barney have reasonably relied on Bodenhorn's assurances that the fabric was flame retardant, or should he have determined the material's flame characteristics for himself? Moreover, even if Barney didn't know that locking the doors was dangerous, the jury might conclude that he should have known and was therefore guilty.

Barney either knew or should have known that his actions and omissions were "wanton or reckless." They had him coming and going.

Just how well the jurors followed these fine points can never be clear. However, after the judge had completed his formal charge, Callahan rose to press Judge Hurley to clarify certain matters for the jury. Acceding to several of the requests, the judge made some "clarifications," but he did Barney no favors. For instance, Callahan asked the judge to address the effect of inspections by public authorities on Barney's legal responsibility. The judge told the jurors that they could consider these inspections to determine Barney's state of mind. Nevertheless, he added, "If these officials were derelict, that would not excuse . . . willful and wanton conduct."

At 2:30 in the afternoon, the jurors retired to deliberate the fate of three men charged with killing nineteen people. There was the testimony of 137 witnesses to consider and 155 exhibits to review, including the numerous photographs taken after the fire, the charred imitation palm tree, scorched Venetian doors and EXIT signs, the remnants of the various other doors, and fragments of fabric and electrical wiring.

The expectation was that deliberations would take several days. However, four hours and fifty minutes later, at 7:20, the foreman of the jury, salesman Joseph S. Murray, knocked on the door of the jury room to get the attention of the court clerk. The jury had reached its verdicts. The speed of the deliberations had surprised the regular observers, and the courtroom was sparsely populated when Judge Hurley reconvened the proceedings at 7:55 P.M.

Court clerk Martin Lee asked the defendants and the jurors to stand. The name of the first alleged manslaughter victim listed in the indictments, Mary H. Duggan, was read. Lee asked the foreman, "What do you say to Barnett Welansky?" Murray answered quietly, "Guilty." "As to James Welansky?" "Not guilty," answered Murray. "As to Jacob Goldfine?" Murray answered again, "Not guilty." Lee then went down the list of the other eighteen victims in the indictments, ending with fifteen-year-old Eleanor Chiampa. Each time foreman Murray's response was the same.

Barney accepted the verdicts—guilty of nineteen counts of involuntary manslaughter—without any sign of emotion. Jimmy and Goldfine, who could not be sure of their fates until they had heard "not guilty" nineteen times, were told by Judge Hurley that they were free to go. They both cried.

In certain respects, the judge's instruction had let Jimmy and Goldfine off the hook. He had told the jurors, "You are to find" that fixtures and decorations were installed solely under Barney's supervision and direction. "And whatever you find . . . about the fixtures, decorations, and light will have no bearing on the guilt of James Welansky or Jacob Goldfine." Their responsibility for these installations was limited, the judge instructed, to whether they "saw conditions there which should have suggested to them a great danger to the public."

Jimmy's tears after hearing the verdicts no doubt reflected both his personal relief and devastation over his brother's multiple convictions. The jury had bought Jimmy's defense that he didn't know much about the operation of the Grove and that he was there on the night of the fire out of filial loyalty. Bushnell had never been able to get much traction out of Jimmy's assurance to the licensing board that all was "according to Hoyle."

The indictment of Goldfine, the wine steward, had from the beginning been widely viewed as a curiosity. His lawyer, Abraham Webber, had successfully depicted him as "little more than an errand boy," despite the prosecution's hints that he was more. Bushnell had tried, unsuccessfully, to elicit testimony that Goldfine had a financial interest in Jimmy's Circle Lounge Bar in Brighton. Moreover, Goldfine had admitted at the Reilly hearings that he was the custodian of the keys to the locked doors. None of this had stuck. On his way out of the courtroom, through his tears, Goldfine lamented his boss's fate. "He doesn't deserve it," he said. "It's too tough a rap."

Barney was free to leave as well. His bail was doubled to $20,000, which was promptly pledged by the bail bondsman whom Callahan had waiting in the courtroom, most likely because he anticipated the bad news. Welansky was free at least until the following Thursday, April 15, when he would be sentenced. The sentence could range from probation to 20 years for each count—180 years.

On the following Thursday, Herbert Callahan sprang into action at the sentencing hearing. First, he announced to the court that he had assembled eighteen character witnesses to testify on Barney's behalf, including several bank executives, lawyers, and businessmen. The judge declined to hear their testimony, stating that he knew what these witnesses would say.

Callahan then made his plea for a lenient sentence. After reciting Barney's rags-to-riches biography, he repeated the arguments he had made in his jury summation, which by this time must have been wearing thin. He concluded with the statement, "I ask your honor to treat Barnett Welansky here as a technical defendant, certainly not as a felon. I leave Barnett Welansky in your hands."

Attorney General Robert Bushnell saved his most explosive—and most intriguing—outburst for this moment. No longer constrained by the formal rules of evidence and jury-trial procedure, Bushnell proceeded full-bore and at full voice. He directed his anger evenly at Welansky and at those who had come out of this scandal untouched so far.

Bushnell seized on Callahan's characterization that Barney's guilt was only a "technical thing." This constituted, Bushnell shouted, "libels or slanders on the dead." The Grove, he said, "was diabolically designed to lure people into blind alleys, blocked passageways, with doors locked . . . just so that the click of the cash register could be heard. I think this is not a technical offense." He added, "More lives were snuffed out in the Cocoanut Grove on November 28 than in many of the largest [German blitzkrieg] raids on England in 1940."

Everyone knew, he said, that the Grove was "the product of the underworld" and that nevertheless "Welansky was kowtowed to as a big shot by newspapers and bankers."

Then Bushnell began unraveling the mystery of the "free list." Some newspapers had speculated that there was a standing list of influential people who did not pay for dinners and drinks at the Grove. "There was no set, fixed free list," he said. "It wasn't done that way." Bushnell explained that the name of a customer was put on a check for liquor or food and the cost charged on the books as an operating expense. The names of newspapermen, police captains, and "other officials, some having to do with laws affecting places like the Grove," appeared on these checks "again and again," he told the court. (After the checks were discovered several days after the fire, reporters asked a Massachusetts State Police detective about the names written on them. He replied that they were "names . . . you'll not ask how to spell when you hear them.")

Although there was no standing free list, a diary was discovered in the ruins of the Grove, said Bushnell. The little book contained telephone numbers and obscure references to important people. He offered Barney the opportunity to decipher these entries "to put an end to the hypocrisy, fraud, and sham. I'd like to try all of them, high and low, and let your honor deal with them."

Bushnell allowed that others shared the guilt, that Barney was both perpetrator and scapegoat. "Barnett Welansky could not alone have created these conditions," shouted Bushnell. "He is a sort of product of these conditions, isn't he, rather than their creator? The people he thought were his friends because they let him get away with it have actually brought him here."

The attorney general suggested that Barney could have saved himself but had not: "If his attitude had been different, he would be in another position here. He stands at the bar now as one who has shown not the slightest disposition to help prevent another such calamity." He invited Welansky to deal, even at this late date: "Callahan says his client was not alone responsible. We agree. . . . If all the laws had been enforced by all the officials, I believe Welansky would not be in the dock today. . . . All right Mr. Welansky, I say to you . . . instead of blaming the dead for the killing, come forward and we are willing to listen to you. . . . We would like to know some things that only Mr. Welansky knows."

With the hearing closed, Barney would now learn his fate. Judge Hurley instructed the Court Clerk Martin Lee to read the sentence:

> The court sentences you on each count to not less than 12 years nor more than 15 years in state prison, to be served concurrently, the first 24 hours to be spent in solitary confinement and the residue at hard labor.

Under the sentence, Barney would not be eligible for parole for eight years. At a minimum, he would be incarcerated at least until 1951.

The indefatigable Callahan asked the judge to allow Barney to remain free pending the outcome of an appeal, which he had already filed. Judge Hurley explained that under state law he could not stay the execution of the sentence unless he filed a certificate stating that it was his opinion that there was reasonable doubt about the defendant's guilt. "I have been unable to form such an opinion," said the judge, "and therefore I cannot file a certificate. I deny the motion for stay of sentence."

Barney was then handcuffed and transported to the old gray state penitentiary in Charlestown. There, he was placed into solitary confinement, presumably to spend 24 hours reflecting on his crime and the enormity of its consequences.

The newspapers reported that, wearing his drab gray inmate's uniform, Barnett C. Welansky sat down that evening to a meal of corned beef hash, bread, and tea.

CHAPTER 15

Reckonings

Put not your trust in princes.

Psalms 146:3

THERE IS A STORY—perhaps apocryphal—about Mayor Maurice J. Tobin and the Cocoanut Grove fire that may have circulated among reporters but never made its way to the newspaper pages.

Nineteen-year-old Mary McCormack died at the Grove. Mary was the daughter of Edward "Knocko" McCormack, a South Boston bar owner and local political powerhouse. Befitting his business and nickname, Knocko was a big, beer-bellied, cigar-chomping tough guy. He was also the brother of John McCormack, Speaker of the U.S. House of Representatives.

The story goes that the mayor visited Mary's wake and attempted to express his condolences to Knocko, who would have none of it. The grieving father believed that the mayor bore some responsibility for his daughter's death. According to this story, Knocko brushed aside Tobin's outstretched hand and punched the mayor in the face.

If this story is true, this was the only price Maurice J. Tobin ever paid for the Cocoanut Grove fire.

In 1944, two years after the fire, Tobin was elected governor of Massachusetts. During the campaign, there was no mention of the Grove fire and his rumored near indictment. Upon his election to higher office, he resigned as mayor with one year left to his term. After an undistinguished term as governor, he lost the office in the postwar national Republican sweep of 1946. President Truman then appointed him Secretary of Labor, a post in which he earned a reputation as a pro-union advocate and committed liberal.

On a Sunday morning in July 1953, following a call to his local church to ask whether his wife could receive Holy Communion after she had ingested two aspirin, Maurice J. Tobin suffered a fatal heart attack. He was fifty-one years old.

In 1945, William Arthur Reilly, adhering to the plan of succession, ran for mayor with Tobin's blessing and support. His main opponents were John E. Kerrigan and the ubiquitous James Michael Curley, who was hoping for yet another political comeback. Kerrigan, the president of the City Council, had been named acting mayor in 1944 to serve the one year left of Tobin's unexpired term, and now he sought to win the office in his own right. There were also three dark horse candidates.

Reilly tied himself to the Tobin "reform" tradition. He argued repeatedly that this was a two-man race and that only he stood between James Michael Curley and a City Hall of renewed corruption. However, there was some evidence that this line had worn thin. The Republican *Herald* had opposed Tobin's run for governor in 1944, suggesting that there was not much difference between him and Curley after all. By 1945, the paper appeared to have lost all faith. Alluding to Tobin and Reilly's dapper images, the paper's political analyst opined that "events of the last eight years have distinctly discredited the fashion plate type of Mayor."

Nevertheless, Reilly had the support of most of the Boston establishment—it had nowhere else to go and saw him as another bulwark against Curley. In a tone reminiscent of its pro-Tobin editorials eight years earlier, the *Boston Post* told its readers that "to elect anyone except Mr. Reilly . . . would be to let down the various groups of able citizens who have got together . . . to plan for the postwar future of this city." The *Post* was shameless in its pro-Reilly coverage. It ran daily stories under headlines like "More Veterans Turn to Reilly," "Surge to Reilly," "Reilly Gets Ovation in East Boston," "Businessmen Hail Reilly as New Mayor," "Jewish Leaders Support Reilly," "Knights of Columbus Head for Reilly." The *Post* tended to acknowledge Curley only when it reported Reilly's attacks on him.

In addition, acting Mayor Kerrigan quickly frittered away the advantages of his incumbency. Early into his one-year term, the acting mayor disappeared. There was no sign of or word from Kerrigan for several weeks. City Hall issued an explanation for his absence. The voters were reminded that he had valiantly led the city through a brutal winter season of clogged thoroughfares and fuel oil shortages. As a result, it was explained, Kerrigan was exhausted by the strains of office, and he was virtually forced by friends, staff, and doctors to go south for a rest. Nevertheless, said state representative John E. Powers, his campaign manager, "he had been wrestling with an idea—a vision—his recreation project. He decided to take his rest," said Powers, "and at the same time get as much information as he could on playground and recreation equipment."

Acting Mayor John E. Kerrigan was at last tracked down. He was indeed pursuing his "vision"—a chorus girl whom he had met in Boston and followed down to New Orleans.

Kerrigan's candidacy seemed doomed, making Reilly a sure winner. Nevertheless, Reilly was dogged throughout the campaign by questions about the Grove fire. Earlier in 1945, Executive Councilor John J. Sawtelle, who would later enter the mayoral race in his own right, led the successful opposition to Reilly's appointment as head of the Metropolitan District Commission, a post to which he had been nominated by his pal, now Governor Maurice Tobin. The commission was the state authority that administered large-scale public works projects. Sawtelle cited the Grove fire as the basis for his opposition. "Mr. Reilly may not have been legally responsible . . . ," he said, "but there is a moral and inescapable obligation that argues powerfully against promoting him to a position of wider responsibility." As a mayoral candidate, Sawtelle would constantly remind voters that Reilly had controlled the fire department for a considerable period before the Grove fire occurred.

"Political Experts See Reilly Victory," the *Post* announced two days before the election. The story under the headline dismissed a report that Curley was leading in the polls, calling it "an old political trick in an effort to influence those voters who like to be with a winner." This "news" story assured readers that those in the know were predicting that Reilly was "certain of winning by a handsome plurality."

When the returns were in, Reilly ran a poor third to Curley, who won by a landslide. He even ran behind John E. Kerrigan, who got one-third again as many votes as Reilly. The former fire commissioner carried just one Boston district—his own "two-toilet Irish" community of West Roxbury.

The anti-Curley vote had splintered among Kerrigan, Reilly, and three others, but why had Reilly run a poor third?

In an editorial that appeared the day after the election, the *Herald* expressed surprise at his miserable electoral performance. "His earlier intimacy with Mr. Curley and his close association with Governor Tobin may not have helped," but those ties alone did not explain his poor showing in the paper's view. "Does the Cocoanut Grove horror account in part for his meager total?" the editorial asked. "Without believing he was at fault in any way," it went on, "the voters may have concluded that somebody was, that nobody had been punished sufficiently and that here was an opportunity to say quietly that they wanted to hit somebody. Mr. Reilly was the most inviting target."

Although he would never again run for office, Reilly continued in politics as the highway commissioner for three-term Boston Mayor John Hynes, who succeeded Curley in 1949. Chastened by his experience, he told his family that he would take any public post except fire commissioner because he never again wanted to bear the responsibility of that life-and-death position. He died in 1969 at the age of sixty-six.

When the New Year's Eve indictments were announced, Attorney General Robert Bushnell promised more. He said that the commonwealth's investigation "into the question of criminal responsibility for the Cocoanut Grove disaster is not ended and will not end until all available avenues of inquiry along this line have been covered." Moreover, during his outburst at Barney's sentencing hearing, he had reiterated his threat to "try all of them, high and low."

Curiously, however, after the Barney Welansky trial, Bushnell lost his ardor. There would be no additional indictments, and the trials of the other defendants were half-hearted efforts. After all, there were no big fish left, and Bushnell had his own political problems.

In July 1943, five defendants accused of conspiracy to violate the building laws were brought to trial—Jimmy Welansky, designer Rueben O. Bodenhorn, building inspector Theodore Eldracher, contractor Samuel Rudnick, and David Gilbert, Rudnick's foreman. Barney had been a defendant in this alleged conspiracy as well, but he was not tried, the prosecutors evidently deciding that they had him where they wanted him.

Eldracher's indictment for failing to report insufficient exits was quashed before the trial as repetitive of the conspiracy charge. The trial judge ordered a directed verdict for Bodenhorn. After hearing testimony for two weeks, the jury acquitted Eldracher, Gilbert, and Jimmy Welansky of conspiracy. The panel had deliberated for ten hours, more than twice the time Barney's jury had taken to find him guilty of involuntary manslaughter.

The jury found Rudnick guilty. Over the years since 1933, Rudnick had supervised the various Melody Lounge renovations as well as the recent construction of the New Broadway Lounge—without many of the required permits. He received a two-year sentence, which was stayed pending appeal. The appellate court confirmed his conviction but recommended that his sentence be suspended. Rudnick never went to prison.

Later, in November 1943, a Suffolk County jury acquitted Lieutenant Frank J. Linney of all charges against him. No doubt thinking of the "condition–good" and "sufficient exits" statements in his infamous report, Linney declined a reporter's invitation to comment on his acquittal. "I guess I've made too many statements already," he said.

Also in November 1943, Building Commissioner James Mooney went on trial for willful neglect of duty in connection with the enforcement of the building laws. The charges resulted from Mooney's statement that he did not have authority to license or supervise the physical condition of nightclubs because they did not charge for admission. At trial, Mooney argued that he was only following the traditional practice and had done what every other building commissioner had. The licensing board, he said, had always regulated all aspects of nightclubs. The licensing board's witnesses before the Reilly inquest had disagreed with Mooney, claiming that the final word on exits and building safety lay with the fire and building departments. Nevertheless, the judge agreed that, at worst, Mooney had misunderstood the scope of his authority and responsibility. The judge ordered a directed verdict of not guilty.

In July 1944, Attorney General Bushnell announced that he was dropping the charges against Captain Joseph A. Buccigross. In explaining his decision to the court, Bushnell said that Buccigross had no special expertise on fire prevention. Moreover, in a tone reminiscent of his earlier pronouncements, he told the court that "officials higher in authority than this defendant" had permitted the Grove to "pack 'em in" without interference. Bushnell went on to quote the grand jury's "indictment" of Boston's officialdom that had accompanied the formal charges, saying that he found those conclusions "sound."

Some time later, the Massachusetts legislature enacted a private bill that awarded the captain all of his back pay. Governor Tobin signed it into law. Buccigross eventually retired with a disability pension based on injuries he claimed to have suffered at the Cocoanut Grove.

Bushnell's crusade to redeem Boston politics had ended with a whimper.

Perhaps he had lost interest in his promised prosecution of the unnamed "higher-ups" because he knew that his days in public life were numbered. In 1944, Governor Leverret Salton-stall would run for the U.S. Senate. His lieutenant governor, Horace T. Cahill, was the Republican candidate to replace Saltonstall, and he was not likely to stick with the difficult Bushnell. The feisty attorney general had proven himself a thorn in Saltonstall's side for four years.

For instance, during the 1943 grand jury proceedings that led to Police Commissioner Timilty's indictment, Bushnell had successfully persuaded the jurors to call on the governor to appear before them, presumably to explain the circumstances of Timilty's appointment, a very tangled subject that the governor certainly did not want to discuss.* Irritated by Bushnell's tweaking, the governor declined the invitation, citing separation of powers. He instead invited the grand jurors to "visit me as citizens."

Furthermore, during the late 1943 controversy over the police department's behavior in connection with the attacks on young Jewish men, Saltonstall's public safety commissioner

---

*At the time, and since the nineteenth century, the governor of the commonwealth appointed the Boston police commissioner. Governor Curley had appointed his ally Timilty to the post during his 1937–1939 term. When he took over in 1940, Governor Saltonstall, a Republican, had kept him on, apparently to keep the peace with Curley. In 1949, Timilty demonstrated his gratitude by running for mayor against Curley.

had placed the blame on rank-and-file police officers. Bushnell fired back that this was typical of the "conventional and accepted policy to place the blame down below." Under pressure from his own attorney general, Saltonstall reluctantly replaced Timilty.

Although it was describing his excesses in connection with the Timilty–Doc Jasper affair, a special crime commission of the Massachusetts State Senate, writing in 1955, made an observation about Bushnell's personality that might be more generally applied:

> By this time [1943], Mr. Bushnell had become a highly controversial figure. . . . Perhaps, as charged, he did . . . go too far, or try too much, or make indiscreet public statements about pending cases. One thing stands out clear. He was the most successful prosecutor of large-scale organized crime in this State, and one of the pioneers in the country in effective sledgehammer blows at the gambling rackets.

Today, Robert T. Bushnell might be described as lacking personal skills. In the '40s, however, among politicians of all stripes, the general assessment was more blunt—the man was simply a pain in the ass.

After his public career ended, Bushnell returned to private practice, both in Boston and New York. He died suddenly of a heart attack in New York City in 1949, while in the midst of his defense of an alleged war profiteer. He was fifty-three. The *Globe* noted in its obituary that he had alienated many people "because of his cleavage to the line he thought right, regardless of friendships." The *Herald* expressed its admiration for him, but added, "He was not, however, a particularly tactful man. . . . A successful political career was not in the cards for him."

In the year of his death in 1994, at the age of sixty-eight, Stanley F. Tomaszewski finally expressed his lifetime of frustration. "I wish people would let a dead horse die," he said. "I've suffered enough—spit on, called every name in the book, threatened, phone calls in the middle of the night. It hasn't been easy."

Stanley had gone on to graduate from Boston College and then spent his working life as a federal auditor. His wife, Betty, said, "He was the father of my three children and a very decent man. . . . The whole thing left a scar on my husband. . . . He even told me about the Cocoanut Grove and what they said about him when he asked me to marry him fifty years ago."

More than fifty years after the fire, the elderly man who had been referred to during the trial as "Little Stanley" protested that he had carefully stomped out the match he had used to find the loosened lightbulb. He pointed out that "none of the investigations say I started the fire." That is true. To this day, the fire is listed as of "unknown origin" in the records of the Boston fire department and the state fire marshall's office. In addition, in the years since, some have clung to other theories of causation: the faulty electrical wiring or the methyl chloride refrigerant used in air conditioners during the war.

However, these alternative theories overlook (as Stanley, the old man, understandably overlooked) that Stanley the youth had been asked by William Arthur Reilly days after the fire, "Do you think the fire started at that palm tree where the light was?" His simple answer was "I think so."

Then there was the immediate testimony of other eyewitnesses, such as Gunner's Mate James W. Lane, who said he saw "a flame about the size of a dinner plate" flashing at the top of the tree. This was the precise location where Stanley had said he had found the loosened lightbulb—an unlikely place for an electrical or gas fire to start. Furthermore, several days after the fire, Barney's nephew Daniel Weiss, the medical student who had worked weekends in the Melody Lounge, testified that he was certain that the fire had started in the palm tree and that he saw several leaves burning "from the middle to the top" of the tree.*

Stanley was not burned in the fire, and he therefore bore no physical marks. However, he was scarred for the rest of his life by the enormous consequences of his momentary lapse. In that sense, Stanley F. Tomaszewski should be counted among the victims of the Cocoanut Grove fire.

Mickey Alpert, a founder of the Cocoanut Grove and its "face man" until its final night, disappeared from Boston shortly after his testimony at the Reilly inquest. Even Barney must not have known his whereabouts. When tenor Billy Payne testified at the trial, Callahan asked him where Alpert was. "In New York," said Payne, "in some hotel." No doubt concerned that Callahan might find some way to blame him, Mickey kept himself at a safe distance from the Boston proceedings.

Mickey was, in a manner of speaking, finally tracked down by author Stephanie Schorow in 2003.** In her book, she recounts

---

*Years later, however, when interviewed for a WGBH piece on the fire, Weiss offered the theory that someone had thrown a lit cigarette into the pot at the base of the palm tree. This theory is inconsistent with every observation—including his own in 1942—that the fire had begun near the top of the tree, or at least as he put it, "from the middle to the top."

**Stephanie Schorow, *Boston on Fire* (Beverly, Mass.: Commonwealth Editions, 2003).

the story of Mickey's post–Cocoanut Grove life as related to her by his daughter Jane. Mickey did go to New York, where he married his girlfriend at the home of comedian Milton Berle. In a bizarre twist, Mickey's wife had been burned severely in another fire.

Thereafter, Mickey worked in the budding television industry as a casting director for such shows as Berle's *Texaco Star Theater*, as well as for the Jackie Gleason and Ed Sullivan shows. Despite a new and relatively successful life, Mickey never overcame his Cocoanut Grove experience. "Sick at heart," wrote Schorow, "he couldn't handle the memories of that horrible night and the accusing eyes of those who wondered why he had survived while their loved ones hadn't." Mickey died in 1965. He was sixty-two years old.

Barney Welansky was disbarred in 1944. In 1945, the federal government tried him and brother Jimmy for tax evasion. They were found guilty and had large judgments imposed against them, but their prison sentences were suspended.

There were hundreds of lawsuits brought against the Grove corporation. Oddly, however, no personal lawsuits were filed against Barney, despite the fact that he had been found criminally liable.

The New Cocoanut Grove Corporation was placed into receivership in order to marshal its assets, the largest of which turned out to be the thousands of cases of liquor—without federal tax stamps—that had been spared by the fire. The Parker House purchased the liquor at auction for $171,000. The receivers had to pay $15,000 of that amount to cover the cost of the missing federal tax stamps.

Jennie Welansky surrendered her "ownership" of the land at 17 Piedmont Street, and the sale of that lot generated about

$15,000. The fire insurance proceeds—Barney had no liability insurance—totaled little more than $20,000.* All told, the New Cocoanut Grove Corporation had assets of approximately $200,000. The federal government claimed well over $100,000 of that sum for taxes due from 1935 to 1941. All of the Grove's commercial creditors waived their claims on condition that the funds be distributed to the surviving victims and the relatives of the dead. Each claimant ultimately received about $150.

The Grove employees received no workers compensation. Such coverage was voluntary for employers in Massachusetts, and Barney had declined.

Meanwhile, Herbert F. Callahan continued the battle on behalf of his friend and partner. First, he petitioned the courts, unsuccessfully, for a reduction of sentence. He also challenged Barney's disbarment, taking the matter all the way up to the Supreme Judicial Court of Massachusetts. Callahan asserted, as he had during the trial, that Barney's violations were "technical," that they had nothing to do with his fitness to practice law. The court affirmed the disbarment in 1946, holding that "the average citizen would find it incongruous" for the state to have adjudicated Barney guilty of manslaughter but entitled to retain his membership in the bar.

Callahan also appealed Barney's conviction to the Supreme Judicial Court, filing an enormous brief that alleged no fewer than 124 "assignments of error" at trial. The court found only five of the alleged errors worthy of discussion. In the course of dismissing several of his contentions, the court rubbed salt in the wound by implicitly questioning Callahan's trial strategy.

---

*No insurance inspector had visited the premises since April 1936. Nevertheless, even the local insurance industry seemed to have deferred to Barney. The Grove's fire insurance rate was less than half the going rate for similar structures in Boston.

First, it held that the jury's visit to the Grove's ruins and the admission of the 102 photographs were not errors. "Any material changes from the conditions before the fire could have been shown by evidence," the court said, suggesting that Callahan had failed to offer such countervailing information.

Callahan had assigned as error the admission of all evidence and testimony concerning Barney's control of the corporation and the premises—such matters as the dummy directors, phantom board meetings, and his obsessive control over all aspects of the Grove's operations. Callahan argued that the cumulative effect of this evidence and testimony had given the jury an unfavorable impression of his character "in matters not relevant to any wanton or reckless conduct." The court pointed out that Barney could have short-circuited much of this unflattering "character" evidence by acknowledging his control early in the trial, rather than waiting until he was on the stand. It was Callahan's own fault if such evidence had prejudiced Barney, the court suggested: "[H]e should blame his own insistence upon trying the case 'closely,' as the phrase is, with respect to a point that he later had to admit."

Callahan reiterated on appeal that only the corporate entity that owned the Grove should have been indicted. There was "nothing" in this point, the court held, adding that Barney "could not escape criminal responsibility by using the corporate form."

The prosecutors were "properly allowed to show" that Barney had not provided the New Broadway Lounge with fusible doors or the unobstructed fire exit to Shawmut Street, as had been indicated in the approved building department plans. "[T]he mode of construction . . . indicated that he did not intend to provide either," the court held.

Callahan won a pyrrhic victory with regard to the testimony and evidence about the Grove's electrical system. The court acknowledged that there was no evidence that the faulty wiring caused the fire, and that "[a] verdict of guilty could not lawfully have been based upon any such defect." Callahan's remedy for this error was to ask the trial court to strike this evidence "when it appeared that no causal relation existed." However, the court noted, "No such request was made."

As to the other 119 assignments of error, the court said they "have not been overlooked. We find nothing in them that requires discussion. Judgments Affirmed."

The court's landmark decision took the law of involuntary manslaughter beyond the narrow realm of driving a car or firing a gun recklessly. No longer was involuntary manslaughter limited to acts that lead directly to the injury or death in question; it now clearly extended to *disregard* for the safety of others to whom one has a duty of care. Moreover, it was not necessary to prove specifically which of the alleged acts or omissions caused the deaths of the victims. Bushnell and Doyle argued, "All of the defendant's acts contributed to the panic . . . and all who died were subjected to flame, heat, smoke and gases of the fire as a result of the combined effects of the defendant's recklessness."

The court agreed. "To convict the defendant of manslaughter," the court held, the state "was not required to prove that he caused the fire. . . . It was enough to prove that death resulted from his wanton or reckless disregard of the safety of patrons in the event of fire from any cause." That wantonness or recklessness could be inferred from what the defendant actually knew about the dangerous conditions or what, from the vantage point of the "reasonable man," he should have known.

This was not an entirely new concept. The Grove case was not the first disaster to result in criminal charges against owners, managers, or even public officials.

The 1911 fire at the Triangle Waist Company in New York caused the death of 147 people, most of them young immigrant factory girls. Many were found behind a locked exit door. The owners were brought to trial on felony manslaughter charges. However, the trial judge told the jurors that they could convict only if they found that the owners *knew* that the exit door was locked. They were acquitted.

The largest public assembly fire death toll in U.S. history occurred in 1903. The fire at the Iroquois Theater in Chicago resulted in 602 deaths, most of them women and children attending a matinee at a theater that had been advertised as fireproof. Charges of negligence were brought against the theater manager, workmen, the fire and building commissioners, and even the mayor. All charges were dismissed. A tavern owner was convicted of robbing the dead victims.

The case of *Commonwealth v. Welansky* moved the law beyond these early cases. It marked the first time an appellate court had so clearly and comprehensively defined the law of involuntary manslaughter, especially in the context of multiple deaths in places of public assembly. The *Welansky* rule has been the basis for manslaughter indictments of the owners of the Station nightclub in West Warwick, Rhode Island, and of the E2 nightclub in Chicago. A fire at the Station in 2003 killed one hundred people. A stampede at the E2, also occurring in 2003, resulted in the deaths of twenty-one people after a security guard used pepper spray to break up a fight in the overcrowded club, causing a panicked rush of several hundred people toward a single available exit. These indictments are still pending.

Barney was diagnosed with terminal cancer of the lung and trachea in early 1946, about three years into his prison term.

He was periodically taken under guard from prison to Massachusetts General Hospital for treatment, but his prognosis was grim.

The ever-loyal Herbert Callahan petitioned the governor—Maurice J. Tobin—for Barney's release on humanitarian grounds. Tobin was understandably skittish about releasing the man whom political foes had described as an "intimate friend," but he permitted public hearings to be held by the parole board. Some relatives of the victims were magnanimous, like Lawrence Nadeau, brother of Claudia Nadeau O'Neil, who had died with her new husband, their best man, and maid of honor in the Grove barely three hours after their marriage. He did not hold Barney responsible for the deaths, Nadeau said, and he favored clemency. "City officials are to blame. . . . Why should one man suffer when there are others to blame?" said Nadeau. Pauline Seider, a sister of another Grove victim, was not so generous. She believed that "Welansky should die like a rat in jail." Mrs. Mary Connell, who lost her son, said, "If this man is pardoned, is that justice?" A doctor testified, "I wouldn't be surprised if he dies tomorrow."

In late November of 1946, having lost his re-election bid for governor and therefore immunized from political reprisal, Tobin quietly permitted Barney's release. Technically, the release was approved by the Governor's Executive Council, by a five-to-four vote. Council member John J. Sawtelle, who had opposed Arthur Reilly's appointment to head the Metropolitan District Commission, voted for the pardon.

When informed of the pardon, Welansky is reported to have said quietly, "That's fine." He was released on November 26, 1946—two days shy of the fourth anniversary of the fire and four days after his forty-ninth birthday. He had served three years and seven months. The feeble, emaciated man who walked out of the low-security Norfolk Prison Colony was bitter. "If you were wrongfully convicted—framed—you'd feel you had a perfect right to be free," he told reporters.

Then he added, "I only wish I had been at the fire and died with those others."

Barney died in March 1947, taking all of his secrets to the grave. He never took up Bushnell's offer to deal for leniency in return for telling "some things that only Mr. Welansky knows."

The *Herald* reported that eight hundred persons attended his funeral services at the Levine Chapel, "including public officials, friends in the theatrical world and many attorneys."

In June 1945, the police discovered that someone had broken into the fenced-in remains of the Grove. The intruder had then taken down a portion of the brick wall of the Melody Lounge, behind which was hidden a huge Mosler safe. Its lock had been expertly drilled out and the contents removed. This final Cocoanut Grove mystery was never solved.

The building was torn down in September 1945. Since then, the site has been radically reconfigured by modern super-block development that truncated Broadway. It is now the site of the twenty-story Boston Radisson Hotel. At the back of the hotel, next to a loading platform, is a small bronze plaque stating that the building is on the site of the Cocoanut Grove nightclub, where nearly five hundred people died in the fire that occurred there on November 28, 1942.

CHAPTER 16

Fact or Fiction?

It's too good to be true.

Everyday expression

WHEN PEOPLE STRUGGLE to comprehend enormous events, it is almost inevitable that they will search for comfort in neat vignettes that demonstrate the best and the worst of what they believe about their fellow humans. There are several Coconut Grove stories that may contain some grains of truth, but parables require more than just the facts. They require a moral, which is sometimes hard to extract from the unadorned truth.

What follows are some stories that have become part of the body of the lore of the Cocoanut Grove fire.

First, there is the story, already related here, of Knocko McCormack punching the Teflon Mayor Tobin and thereby exacting payback for his daughter's death—small payback, but very satisfying on a gut level.

Then, there are the unlikely stories of heroism. Take, for instance, Buck Jones, whom millions had seen on the screen invariably demonstrating courage and American decency. How could this Western hero, who hailed from Indiana, this champion of the good and right have died as pitifully as did fifteen-year-old Eleanor Chiampa?

Not surprisingly, Buck's death was national news. More surprising was the story worthy of Buck's own B movie scripts that began circulating in California. According to this version of events, Buck had made it out of the Grove unscathed. Nevertheless, just as his on-screen persona would have done, he had gone back in repeatedly to save his fellow patrons. Then the fire and fumes finally took him down. His screen partner, "Colonel" Tim McCoy, said, "He died saving others. That's what got us through our grief."

As compelling as this story is, it could not be true. Buck Jones was found clinging to life on the terrace where he had been seated all evening. If he had gotten out of the building safely and returned to save others, the likelihood of his falling in the precise spot where he had been seated is extraordinarily small. In addition, the casualty rate on the terrace was particularly large. Those who didn't die on the spot reported afterward that they were immediately overcome by fumes, flames, or the panicked crowd.

In fact, journalist Marty Sheridan, who was freelancing as Jones's Boston public relations handler, wrote in 1995 that his own experience on the terrace belied the saga of Jones's heroism: "When the flames, fumes and smoke hit us I passed out and later came to on the floor. Shock had already set in and there was no way I could have gotten to my feet and attempted to rescue my wife [Constance Sheridan, who died in the Grove] or anyone else."

Then there are the stories of greed tempered by virtue. For example, there is the story of Buck Jones's personal manager

Scotty Dunlop. Scotty had been sitting near Buck when the fire reached the terrace, and the smoke immediately overwhelmed him. Unconscious, he was carried outside by rescuers and dumped onto the cold sidewalk among the dead and near dead.

He came to long enough to hear the voices of men sorting through the piles of bodies to separate the living from the dead. Terrified that he might be counted among the dead and ignored, he picked up his head and mustered the strength to call to one man, alerting him that he was indeed alive.

"I'll give you three hundred dollars to get me to the hospital right away," he was supposed to have told a man whose face he couldn't make out through the darkness. The man asked him where the money was, and Dunlop told him, "It's in my wallet." Then Scotty slipped again into unconsciousness.

Dunlop woke up some time later in Boston City Hospital, suffering from pulmonary edema. Eventually, as the buildup of fluid in his lungs gradually abated, Dunlop asked about his wallet. When it was given to him, he found to his surprise that it contained over five hundred dollars. He had gone into the Grove with slightly more than eight hundred. The mercenary but scrupulous Samaritan had taken the bargained-for sum but had left the correct change.

In addition to wondering about the rescuer, one might ask about Dunlop's ethics in paying to be rescued before some others. On a practical level, one might speculate about the process by which Dunlop had made the snap determination that his life was worth precisely three hundred dollars, rather than four, five, or the entire eight hundred. Was this a time to be bargain shopping?

Then there are the stories that have it all—chorus girls, narrowly escaping entombment at the Grove, and then running through the city in skimpy outfits in a desperate search for their missing lovers or husbands. Never give up!

Pepper Russell and Connie Warren were among the chorus girls trapped for a time in the second-floor dressing room above the stage area. There are two versions of what happened to Pepper, one by Edward Keyes,* another by Paul Benzaquin.** Both versions agree that most of the young dancers, including Pepper and Connie, went down the stairs through the choking and blinding smoke, each with one hand covering her mouth and nose, the other on the shoulder of the girl in front, and that they escaped through the service door to Shawmut Street.

Once safely out of the Grove, Connie and Pepper became concerned about the safety of their men, Connie for her husband, Bill, a Grove cashier, and Pepper for her boyfriend, saxophonist Al Willet. They searched desperately through the crowd outside the burning building, but they could not find Bill or Al. Bill was already dead. According to Benzaquin, Connie was "unaware that he had died in a desperate rush across the Dining Room to save her." The name of William H. Warren does in fact appear on the official record as "Dead, Southern Mortuary." However, just whom Benzaquin interviewed about the dead man's "desperate rush" to save his wife is unclear.

Red Cross workers wrapped the two women in blankets and took them to a room in the Bradford Hotel, which had made its facilities available to Grove employees. Both the Keyes and Benzaquin versions have Pepper unable to sleep, but Benzaquin's version is much more dramatic: "She had barely begun to

---

*Edward Keyes, *The Cocoanut Grove* (New York: Atheneum, 1984)

**Paul Benzaquin, *Holocaust!* (New York: Holt, 1959).

relax when, suddenly, she felt every muscle in her body respond to a new sensation of shock. It was a man's hand on her knee, and moving." She screamed and was saved by two men, who "pounced on the lecher and shoved him out of the room."

In any event, both versions now have a restless Pepper leaving the Bradford and resuming her search for Al Willet. She finds him at Boston City Hospital, in a bed (Benzaquin) or at the Southern Mortuary across the street (Keyes). Here Keyes outdoes Benzaquin: After inquiring at the hospital desk for Willet, Pepper is directed to the mortuary. She goes through the "dingy corridor" connecting the hospital to the mortuary as "orderlies hurried past wheeling hand wagons stacked with inert forms." Pepper enters the mortuary where a priest asks her—gently as priests invariably do—"Do you have someone here?" She didn't know, she answered. Exactly at that moment, an orderly shouts, "This one's alive!" Pepper looks over and screams, "Oh my God! It's Al! It's a miracle father! A miracle!"

Benzaquin's version resumes the chronology, telling the reader that, after a long stay at Boston City Hospital, Al Willet recovered from his pulmonary injuries. He also stopped smoking.

Aside from the too-neat juxtaposition of good and bad outcomes, respectively, for Pepper and Connie and the suspicious melodrama of Pepper's discovery of Al, there is at least one other curiosity about both these versions. William Arthur Reilly's report, issued a full year after the fire, claimed to have listed the names of all of the injured admitted to hospitals, as well as the names of all of the dead. The name Al Willet (or Willette in Benzaquin's version) is not on the list, nor is any reasonable spelling variation of the name. While it is possible that Al Willet was a professional name, and therefore he appears on

the list under his real name, the likelihood of a sideman saxophonist adopting a stage name seems remote. On the other
hand, Pepper Russell's real name was Henrietta Siegel.

There are numerous other dubious Grove stories, but none is
as enduring as the one that goes that the Boston licensing board
has a rule prohibiting the use of the name Cocoanut Grove by
any establishment under its jurisdiction. Why anyone in Boston
would want to name its establishment after a tragedy is unclear.
However, it is evidently legal to do so. According to a licensing
board representative,

> The Board does not have a regulation prohibiting the use of
> that name. I also checked with the City Clerk's Office to see if
> they knew of a City Ordinance prohibiting that use. They were
> not aware of any such ordinance.

The 90-Second Fire

West Warwick, Rhode Island, February 20, 2003

The Station nightclub was no Cocoanut Grove. For starters, Grove maître d' Angelo Lippi would have frowned and turned away its beer-guzzling, jeans-clad habitués. On the other hand, more than sixty years had passed, and nearly everything had changed—or had it?

The Station's fifty-seven-year-old wood building sat at the rear of its parking lot, next to Knight's Garage and the local Nissan dealership. The murals painted across the front of the building set the club's tone with the likenesses of Elvis, Janis Joplin, Jimi Hendrix, Ozzy Osbourne, and Steven Tyler superimposed on the stars and stripes. Inside there were neither palm trees nor billowy satin ceilings nor stiffly uniformed wait staff. Instead, there were pool tables, a dart room, and a large horseshoe-shaped bar with bartenders in sweatshirts. There was no fancy art deco marquee on Cowesett Avenue—only a painted road sign with plastic-letter inserts that spelled out the weekly lineup.

Mondays at the Station were usually karaoke nights, and another slow evening might be "Sumo wrestling night"—white, working-class guys grappling with each other in padded suits. Thursdays were pounding music nights.

That Thursday, the featured band was Great White, a second-tier bluesy metal rock band that had been popular in the eighties. They rarely played the giant gigs in stadiums and arenas anymore, but they had their hard-core fans.

The Station was packed to capacity—or perhaps just slightly over capacity. The town's fire department had, in recent years, increased the club's legal limit from 225 to 404 persons—if as on this night, there were few tables and chairs. There might have been as many as 458 fans and employees there that night, almost all them in their twenties and thirties. Most had come from the immediate area, but a good number had driven from nearby towns just over the Massachusetts or Connecticut lines.

Shortly after 11 P.M. the lights were turned down, and Great White appeared on the bandstand. Front man Jack Russell signaled the start of the music, and the band launched its opening number to appreciative applause, whistles, shouts, and hands raised with "V" signs. This crowd was pumped. Tonight's set might include the song "Rock Me," with the lines, "Before the mornin' light, we'll burn with love tonight. . . ."

The drama of the moment was enhanced by fluttering multicolored lights and four "glebs"—pyrotechnic devices that emitted showers of white sparks.

In keeping with the band's regular practice, one of the musicians might stick his head in the shower to create a harmless halo effect. However, on this night, it took less than ten seconds for the bouncing sparks to ignite the polyurethane acoustical foam that lined the drummer's alcove. Seconds later, the flames spread to the stage area itself. Nonetheless, the band kept playing for nearly half a minute, and most of the fans, thinking that the fire was part of the show, wasted those precious thirty seconds.

As the flame and smoke began to build, the band finally stopped, and the panic started. Most of the crowd headed for the main entrance as the smoke, heat, and gases built up around them. People coming from several directions collided at the door, and it became jammed within ninety seconds.

At that ninety-second point, a layer of black smoke had dropped from the ceiling to about 3 feet above the floor, and the smoke billowed out of the main entrance over the heads of the crushed crowd. Between four and five minutes after the polyurethane had caught fire, flames were licking out of the main entrance door, and the smoke had dropped to about 1 foot above the floor. By the five-minute mark, however, it was much too late for most still inside. Ninety-six people were killed immediately, including the band's guitarist, Ty Longley, and four more died subsequently. Burns, respiratory injuries, or trauma from trampling injured more than two hundred.

There were tools and resources available that did not exist when the Grove burned, and the Station fire was analyzed as perhaps no other public assembly fire had ever been.

The National Institute of Standards and Technology (NIST), an agency of the U.S. Department of Commerce, conducted an exhaustive two-year study of the chemistry of the fire. NIST released its draft report in March 2005. It demonstrated the incredible speed with which a fire can move and the precious few seconds that people have to plan and execute their escapes.

Such devices as cone calorimeters, infrared photography, thermocouples, video cameras, heat flux gauges, bi-directional probes, and gas extraction probes measured the heat release rates of polyurethane foam, wood paneling, acoustical tile, and other materials in the Station, as well as the density of smoke and gases generated by the burning of these materials.

First, NIST created a full-scale mock-up of approximately 20 percent of the Station with polyurethane foam–covered walls, a drummer's alcove, a raised platform, carpeting, and wood paneling.

By conducting ignition tests on the mock-up, NIST was able to estimate the "tenability" of the Station during the fire. A room is deemed untenable for people when *any* of the following occurs: the temperature is greater than 250 degrees Fahrenheit, the rate of heat transfer exceeds tolerable levels, the oxygen volume drops below 12 percent, or the concentrations of hydrogen cyanide or carbon monoxide exceed their LCLo—"lethal concentration low levels," the lowest concentration of those gases known to have caused death.

Tests were conducted in a mock-up without a sprinkler system. This was a realistic test since the Station had none. It had been "grandfathered" under the law that would have required new buildings of its size to have a sprinkler system.

The test results were sobering. In the mock-up without sprinklers, the tenable temperature was exceeded in less than 76 seconds, and the heat transfer rate surpassed tolerable levels in about 60 seconds. The oxygen volume dropped below 12 percent in less than 87 seconds. The hydrogen cyanide reached its lethal concentration low level in less than 75 seconds, the carbon monoxide in less than 92 seconds. The NIST report concluded,

Given the rapid spread of the fire and combustion products, it is likely that the victims succumbed to multiple conditions [heat transfer rate, temperature, lack of oxygen, the hydrogen cyanide, carbon monoxide or smoke levels, or to the crush of the crowd]. If conditions developed in The Station in the same manner as during this mock-up, most occupants likely would have had less than 90 seconds to escape under tenable conditions.

The differences in the sprinklered test of the mock-up were striking. The same mock-up with activated sprinklers was able to maintain tenable conditions—bearable levels of temperature, gases, heat transfer—at head height for the entire five-minute duration of the test, suggesting that if there had been a sprinkler system, the chances were excellent that no one would have died at the Station that night.

To supplement the mock-up studies, NIST also conducted computer simulations of the fire by plugging into its computers data on all of the known variables of the building's construction and materials. The simulation showed that temperature change in the area adjacent to the entryway rose to 1,000 degrees centigrade—1,830 degrees Fahrenheit—in 90 seconds.

The choking, gaseous smoke and the unbearable temperatures enveloped the Station patrons. These computer models suggest the fate of the Cocoanut Grove patrons running and crawling through similar blackness in search of exits that did not exist.

The results in the sprinklered computer simulation were strikingly similar to the results of the mock-up test with sprinklers, reinforcing the idea that all of the Station patrons could have escaped unharmed if there had been a sprinkler system installed. The NIST report concluded, "In the simulation of the full nightclub equipped with sprinklers ... tenable conditions would have existed over the duration of the simulation (300 seconds), as the fire was fully extinguished approximately 114 seconds after ignition."

The NIST study was aided considerably by the videotape of the fire made by a Providence television station cameraman who was taping inside the club on the night of the fire. The pictures of the crowd before and during the early stages of the fire provided a real-time check on NIST's various re-creations of the events. Newsman Jeffery Derderian had given the cameraman the assignment. Derderian, who worked for station WPRI, had developed a reputation for hard-hitting stories. He was in the middle of a piece about nightclub safety, a subject that had generated interest only three days before the fire when twenty-one people were trampled to death in the E2 nightclub in Chicago. The videotape would have been a journalistic coup for Derderian except for the fact that he, along with his brother Michael, was the co-owner of the Station.

Two days after the fire, Jeffrey Derderian sobbed at a news conference and said that the fire was "a horror that will haunt me for the rest of my life." The newsman so used to demanding answers refused to take questions. However, he vehemently denied giving permission for the pyrotechnics that ignited the fire.

Great White's tour manager, Daniel Biechele, disagreed, claiming that he had discussed the pyrotechnics with Michael Derderian, who had given his permission.

Under the *Welansky* theory of reckless disregard, the Derderian brothers and the Great White tour manager, Daniel Biechele, were each indicted on two hundred counts of involuntary manslaughter—two counts per victim. The trials on those charges may not occur until 2006.

In addition, the Derderians' company was fined more than one million dollars because of their failure to have required workers' compensation insurance for its employees. A move by the state to hold them personally responsible for these fines is pending.

The social costs of the fire were staggering. Perhaps as many as sixty-five children lost a parent, and one child lost both.

Then there are the personal and financial burdens. For instance, one survivor, treated at Massachusetts General Hospital, which has become renowned for its burn treatment facilities since the Grove fire, underwent scores of surgeries. This man has lost his fingers, part of his nose, both ears, and his left eye. The health care costs for this one patient are estimated to be several million dollars.

Lawsuits, perhaps ultimately numbering in the hundreds, began to be filed shortly after the disaster. Defendants include the Derderian brothers, Great White, Daniel Biechele, the company that had sold the soundproofing material, the West Warwick fire marshal, the town of West Warwick, the State of Rhode Island, and the state fire marshal.* The town of West Warwick faces huge tax increases and perhaps bankruptcy if it is found liable.

The NIST study of the Station fire made the following recommendation for nightclubs, many of which might be applied to all places of public assembly.

---

*Many of the survivors and relatives of those killed believe that public officials who had not raised questions about the polyurethane foam or who had permitted the occupancy load to increase to over four hundred should also have been indicted. David Kane, father of Nicholas O'Neill, who at age eighteen was the youngest victim of the fire, wrote in the *Providence Journal* that he was disappointed that the grand jury had returned "only three indictments, not one naming a public official . . . it seemed obvious to me that the 'fix was in.'"

- Require automatic fire sprinkler systems for all new and existing nightclubs regardless of size.
- Ban all materials that are not fire retardant, such as polyurethane foam.
- Ban the use of pyrotechnic devices, except in the largest venues, and then only with the strictest controls.
- Calculate the required number of exits based on the assumption that one will be unavailable during an emergency.
- Increase the capacity of exits. The main exit should accommodate two-thirds of the maximum number of people permitted.
- Provide illuminated exit signs at floor level so that persons crawling under flames and smoke might escape.
- Provide explicit instructions for emergency egress prior to the start of any public event.
- End the practice of "grandfathering" blanket exemptions for older structures. Allow waivers only on a case-by-case basis.
- Increase the number of portable fire extinguishers required. Train staff to use them.
- Improve the training of local fire inspectors.
- Require that owners and staff be properly instructed about what to do in case of fire or other emergencies.

Author's Postscript

Although this book is primarily one that tells a story, I would feel remiss without including the following information.

On the public level, individuals can support stringent fire and building codes and their diligent, competent, and honest enforcement. On a personal level, the National Fire Protection Association's (NFPA) Web site offers the following useful recommendations to persons entering any public building.

Should You Enter?

- Take a good look: Does the building appear to be in a condition that makes you feel comfortable? Is the main entrance wide and does it open outward to allow easy exit? Is the outside area clear of materials stored against the building or blocking exits?

Before You Enter

- Have a communication plan: Identify a relative or friend beforehand to contact in case of emergency and you are separated from family or friends.
- Plan a meeting place: Pick a meeting place outside to meet family or friends with whom you are attending the function. If there is an emergency, be sure to meet them there.

When You Enter

- Locate exits immediately: When you enter a building look for all available exits. Are the exits clearly marked and well lit? Some exits may be in front and some in back of you. Always be prepared to use the exit closest to you. (You may not be able to use the main exit.)
- Check for clear exit paths: Make sure aisles are wide enough and not obstructed by chairs or furniture. Check to make sure your exit door is not blocked or chained. If there are not at least two clearly marked exits or exit paths are blocked, report the violation to management and leave the

building if it is not immediately addressed. Call the local
fire marshal to register a complaint.

- Do you feel safe? Does the building appear to be overcrowded? Are there fire sources such as candles burning,
cigarettes or cigars burning, pyrotechnics, or other heat
sources that may make you feel unsafe? Are there safety
systems in place such as alternative exits, sprinklers, and
smoke alarms? Ask the management for clarification on
your concerns. If you do not feel safe in the building, leave
immediately.

During an Emergency

- React immediately: If an alarm sounds, you see smoke or
fire, or there are other unusual disturbances, immediately
exit the building in an orderly fashion. Use your closest
exit—keep in mind that it may not be the main exit.
- Get out, stay out! Once you have escaped, stay out.
Under no circumstances should you ever go back into a
burning building. Let trained firefighters conduct rescue
operations.
- Take the time to learn about the public assembly buildings
you may enter so that you know what to do if the unexpected happens.

Source: NFPA Public Education Division

Some of these precautions might seem excessive or embarrassing to implement. It would be useful to recall that not one
victim of the fires at the Cocoanut Grove and the Station expected to die in those disasters. Far from it. Patrons of both
clubs—though the events were more than sixty years apart—

were there to enjoy themselves. The cautionary words written by NFPA's Robert S. Moulton in his January 1943 report on the Cocoanut Grove fire apply today:

> Fatal fires occur so infrequently in the experience of the average individual that the probability seems too remote to consider—until after the fire, when the picture changes completely and any chance of death by fire, even though it be as slight as one in a million, seems too great a chance to take.

Massachusetts enacted a series of reforms to its fire and building codes in the years immediately following the Grove disaster. More than sixty years later, Rhode Island was roused to take strong action. Because of the public outrage generated by the Station fire, that state now has one of the most stringent public assembly codes in the United States. However, laws by themselves do not prevent public assembly fires. As Massachusetts Attorney General Robert T. Bushnell pointed out in December 1942, "whenever such tragedies occur there is a tendency to look for the cause in defects of statutory law. This has occurred not infrequently when it has been quite obvious that diligent enforcement of the law as it then existed could have prevented the tragedy then under discussion."

Sixty-three years later, Bushnell's words were echoed in connection with the Station fire. On June 29, 2005, NIST released its final report on that tragedy. The first recommendation of the report stated the following: "implement aggressive and effective fire inspection and enforcement programs . . . ensure that enough fire inspectors and building plan examiners are on staff to do the job and that they are professionally qualified."

The preliminary NIST report, released in March 2005, focused on changes to the model codes. However, NIST lead investigator William Grosshandler told the *Providence Journal* that the agency had decided in the interim to emphasize enforcement. "What good does it do to clamp down on a code if it really is an enforcement issue?" Grosshandler told the *Journal*.

Disclosures after the Grove fire established that the city government already had the power to regulate the use of flammable materials, to mandate sufficient exits, and to limit the number of people in places of public assembly. The public servants had the authority but not the will.

Similar questions have been raised about the inspection process as it related to the Station. Why was the flammable foam permitted in the club? Why weren't there more and larger exits? Was the Station overcrowded? These questions may be answered as the criminal and civil litigation proceeds, but one thing is clear: The toughest codes are meaningless unless they are enforced competently, honestly, and free of political interference.

INDEX